Creation Matters

DALE KIEFER

Creation Matters

© 2018 by Dale F. Kiefer

Scripture taken from the NEW AMERICAN STANDARD BIBLE (R), Copyright ©1960, 1962, 1963, 1968, 1971, 1972, 1973, 1975, 1977, 1995 by the Lockman Foundation. Used by permission

ISBN:9781983755248

Design and Layout: Emily Poulin

This book is dedicated to my two wonderful daughters, Elisa and Emily. Their love, thoughtfulness, joy and creativity have been a source of encouragement and motivation for me throughout their lives. They are far better writers than I, so it is with sincere humility that I dedicate this book to them. They truly are reflections of our marvelous Creator.

TABLE OF CONTENTS

IMPLICATIONS

THE CREATOR

Foundation

Anthropology

Cosmology

Geology

Bookends of History

Appendix

ACKNOWLEDGEMENTS

As the author, I accept full responsibility for the contents of this book, which is as it ought to be. The reader will probably discover typos, spelling errors, and assorted other blunders. None of these should be attributed to the great people who assisted me with the book. However, on the positive side, their contributions have guided me through much of what I have written here.

I want to thank:

My friend Clay Clarkson. He wrote some things in an email to me a couple years ago that got me thinking about writing this book. His wisdom, experience in writing books, theological understanding and willingness to challenge some of my ideas have been indispensable, both for how I have written and for getting the book published.

The two people who I mention in the Introduction. With Clay's comments still fresh in my mind, my conversations with them about creation were what motivated me to actually get started writing this book.

My wife, Pat. She encouraged me every step of the way to press on. I have incorporated most of her insights, editorial suggestions and organizational recommendations. Why? Because I love her, which is sufficient reason, but to top it off, she has such good ideas.

My friends Dan and Andie Miller and Kevin Maloney. They were willing to give an amazing amount of time to painstakingly read my drafts and provide meticulous editorial feedback. Their fingerprints are figuratively on every page of the book.

My writers' group colleagues, Jim Poulin and Mark Abel. They, too, gave me valuable editorial feedback, and they continually urged me to keep making progress and to get this work published.

Emily Poulin. This young woman is an extraordinarily gifted graphic artist, and has applied her remarkable skills to the design of not only the book cover but also to the layout of the book.

I just wish everyone could be surrounded by a group of family and friends like these.

We believe in one God,
the Father, the Almighty,
maker of heaven and earth,
of all that is, seen and unseen.

We believe in one Lord, Jesus Christ,
the only Son of God,
eternally begotten of the Father,
God from God,
Light from Light,
true God from true God,
begotten, not made,
of one being with the Father.
Through him all things were made.

Nicene Creed

You cannot truly know God and ignore the doctrine of creation.

Not only that, but if you ignore the doctrine of creation, you cannot truly know Jesus Christ, yourself, others, the world, or the universe. If you ignore the doctrine of creation, you cannot really understand sin, the reason for the Law, salvation, the purpose of life, or our eternal hope. If you ignore creation, you will be hindered in your prayers and in your ability to make sense of the vast variety of life on this earth.

The first thing the Bible tells us about God is this: "In the beginning God created the heavens and the earth," Genesis 1:1. This continues as a prominent theme throughout the entire Bible, right down to the final chapters: "...Him who lives forever and ever, who created heaven and the things in it, and the earth and the things in it, and the sea and the things in it," Revelation 10:6.

I asked an older Christian woman what she thinks about the subject of creation. She responded, "I don't think about it much...I don't think most people do." A few days later I had lunch with a friend, and I mentioned that I was starting to write some studies on creation. His first response was almost verbatim what the woman had said, "You know, I really don't think very much about that."

I have a hunch that their comments represent the sentiment of a large number of Christians. If I am correct, why do hardly any Christians seem to think about creation apart from when they are studying, debating, or discussing creationism vs. evolution?

Perhaps most Christians think of creation as a topic that is confined to Genesis 1-2, and that it receives very little mention in the rest of Scripture. Maybe they also think that it has little relevance to our daily lives or to other doctrines.

The fact is, the doctrine of Creation pervades the Scriptures, being mentioned directly at least 300 times and indirectly hundreds more. This doctrine matters significantly in the Bible, and therefore it should matter to us. It is interwoven into the fabric of the Bible's historical narratives, wisdom literature, law, poetry, prophets, gospels, epistles, and apocalyptic sections. We cannot leave it behind when we get out of Genesis 1-2. Its frequent repetition in the Bible reminds us who God is and how He is working in our lives.

These studies will explore many of the reasons why the doctrine of creation matters. Three of them are worthy of mention as we begin. First, creation matters because it reveals the majesty, wisdom, power and sovereignty of God. Second, as mentioned above, creation matters because it is foundational to many major biblical doctrines. Third, creation matters because many practical implications arise from this doctrine.

The Bible declares repeatedly that we live in a universe created by the one true God. From this perspective, creation is the biblical alternative to naturalistic atheistic explanations for the existence of the universe and life on earth. For all Christians, the doctrine of creation matters greatly.

These studies are intended to help Christians see the significance of the doctrine of creation. The goal is for us to become stronger in our views of it and the topics that depend on it.

We see more than just the fingerprints of God on creation, more than mere evidence of His existence, and more than a manifestation of His power, beauty and wisdom. We are seeing a glimpse of Him. He is separate from His creation. It is external to Him. It is dependent on Him, not vice versa. Nonetheless, He occupies His creation, which is what led King David to remark in Psalm 139:

> *7Where can I go from Your Spirit?*
>
> *Or where can I flee from Your presence?*
>
> *8If I ascend to heaven, You are there;*
>
> *If I make my bed in Sheol, behold, You are there.*
>
> *9If I take the wings of the dawn,*
>
> *If I dwell in the remotest part of the sea,*
>
> *10Even there Your hand will lead me,*

When we look at nature, the heavens and earth, and human beings, we are seeing a revelation of the living God who made, owns, and sustains everything.

Throughout the following studies, I hope that we will see more clearly just how much creation matters. These days it seems that all Christian authors think that any book Introduction necessarily must include a quote from C. S. Lewis. Here I happily continue this tradition.

"No philosophical theory which I have yet come across is a radical improvement on the words of Genesis, that 'In the beginning God made heaven and earth.'"

C. S. Lewis

OVERVIEW

This book can be used for individual or group Bible studies, so I have included response questions at the end of each study. Altogether there are 52 studies, so they can be used for weekly devotionals or Bible study groups that meet weekly.

Studies 1-10 are important implications of the doctrine of creation on how we should think about the world in which we live

Studies 11-28 focus on the Creator, who He is and why we can trust Him.

In **studies 29-34** we will look at how creation is the foundation for several other doctrines in Scripture.

Studies 35-40 deal with biblical anthropology, who we are in light of the doctrine of creation.

In **studies 41-45** we will look at cosmology or what the Bible says about the heavens above and the laws of science that operate in them.

Studies 46-50 examine some biblical teachings about geology, specifically the impact of creation on our view of planet earth.

Finally, **studies 51-52** contains just two studies that focus on the bookends of history, creation and the last days, looking at some key passages concerning how the Bible uses creation as a reference point for much of its narrative, up to and including the climactic future final days of human history.

I have included a brief **Appendix** in which I describe my own position on the age of the earth.

IMPLICATIONS

Studies 1-10 address issues to think about when we think about creation. These studies have a dual purpose: to identify several biblical passages that are central to the doctrine of creation, and to point us toward many more passages that will be explored in studies 11-52.

1

IMPLICATIONS

EVERYTHING IS BEAUTIFUL

*Creation matters because it explains
the existence of beauty.*

When we look around at our natural world, and when we look up at the heavens, we see order, power, life, complexity, simplicity, and mystery. And despite the occasional turbulence and the messes that humans create, we also see beauty.

These are not philosophical constructs; these are realities.

Pop-philosophy says that "beauty is in the eye of the beholder." On one hand that is true. If there are no beholders with eyes, who is to say if there is any beauty? But, the pop-philosophers usually do not mean that. They are trying to point out that things that are beautiful to one person may not be beautiful to someone else. But, is beauty really as subjective as that? I think most people do not really believe it is quite so subjective.

For example, we generally agree on things that are beautiful, although we may differ on the particulars or the degree to which something is beautiful. One person may marvel at the beauty of the mountains, while another may be partial to the beauty of the ocean. Both would admit that the other has its own kind of beauty, and that is precisely where each person agrees with the other, they both acknowledge that there is such a thing as objective beauty. They are not arguing about whether or not there is beauty, but what their preferences are.

The reason Yosemite National Park is nearly overrun each year with visitors is that people agree that the physical features of the park are beautiful. Overall, we humans seem programmed to seek, appreciate and agree on beauty. We prefer it to ugliness, disarray and decay. The artist takes random objects and arranges them on a canvas into an image that depicts the beauty that he or she sees. A poet takes the same words that are available to all of us, and arranges them into a beautiful expression of what he or she envisions. A carpenter takes a random pile of wood and hardware, and creates a beautiful table, chest or chair. In a similar way, the fact that beauty exists in the heavens and on earth is evidence that there is a Creator, one who likes beauty and who has designed us to see and enjoy it. Furthermore, by implication, that Creator is Himself beautiful, because beautiful things are a reflection of some aspect of beauty in their creator. In the case of God the Creator, His beauty is total.

Likewise, order, complexity and intricacy are never the result of randomness. Drop a Home Depot store from 20,000 feet, and when it hits the ground, all that's left is rubble, not a beautiful home with fabulous furnishings and fixtures. Randomness produces chaos, disorder and ugliness. Intelligence, coupled with wisdom and skill produces beauty, order, complexity and intricacy.

The words "beauty" and "beautiful" and their synonyms are used several hundred times in Scripture. They are not used comparatively or subjectively or as opinions. Rather they are simple declarations of fact that God, a thing, or a person is beautiful, and it is understood that everyone would agree. The foundation for beauty is creation itself. In Genesis 1, God declared what He made in each phase of creation to be beautiful, and at the end of the six creation days He declared it all to be beautiful (translated "good" in Genesis 1:31). The original Hebrew word used in Genesis 1 is *tôḇ?*, which is usually translated "good" in that chapter. The word is also translated as "beautiful" many times in the Old Testament, and even when other English words are used to translate it, its root meaning always includes the idea of beauty. The beauty affirmed in Genesis 1 is the basis for all other statements about beauty that will follow in the pages of Scripture. The following are just a handful of the many passages that reflect the reality and objectivity of beauty.

Genesis 1:31

God saw all that He had made, and behold, it was very good [or, "beautiful"].

Genesis 24:16

The girl was very beautiful,

Psalm 27:4

One thing I have asked from the LORD, that I shall seek:
That I may dwell in the house of the LORD all the days of my life,
To behold the beauty of the LORD,
And to meditate in His temple.

Ecclesiastes 3:11

He has made everything beautiful in its time. He has also set eternity in their heart,

Isaiah 28:4

And the fading flower of its glorious beauty,

Isaiah 33:17

Your eyes will see the King in His beauty;

Isaiah 60:13

"The glory of Lebanon will come to you,
The juniper, the box tree and the cypress together,
To beautify the place of My sanctuary;
And I shall make the place of My feet glorious.

RESPOND TO IT

1. Is the idea of objective beauty new to you? How would you differentiate between objective and subjective beauty?

2. What do beauty, order, complexity and intricacy tell us about God?

3. Share one of your memories about one of the most beautiful things you have ever seen in nature and explain why.

2

IMPLICATIONS

OUR WORTH AND SIGNIFICANCE

Creation matters because it explains why we have a sense of worth.

If we come from a long, random, naturalistic process, we have no reason to believe that we have significance or meaning. In that scenario, there is nothing outside us to give us meaning or to provide principles to live by. We and everything else just are. Meaning and significance are contrived constructs, self-assigned by our random, merely material, brains. Any value that we feel or claim to possess comes only and entirely from our selves, but not from a higher Being or purpose outside us. Everyone is only a complex arrangement of inanimate atomic particles, and therefore we have no actual meaning or worth.

But, if we are created, we live in someone else's universe, a universe that is created and governed by that Someone and by the rules, policies and values the Creator has established. Our meaning does not come from ourselves but from Someone outside us. Therefore, our significance is not something that we decide on but something that originates in the One who made us and everything else. It is built into us, and we can sense it, but we do not generate it.

Our inner sense of value transcends the molecules of our brains. Our sense of worth comes because we are more than the atoms that comprise us. We are caused, not uncaused. We are significant, but not ultimate. We feel like we have purpose and meaning because we actually do.

Almost everyone has a deep sense of self-worth. We just know that our lives matter. The underlying truth is, we all are indeed significant, and we know it, we sense it. It is why we eat, why we seek companionship, why we pray, why we cloth ourselves, why we find shelter and comfort, why we protect loved ones and ourselves, why we try to achieve things. Where does that sense of worth come from?

If we are not created, our sense of worth is an illusion, nothing more than an interesting interplay of the atoms, energy, and molecules that comprise our brains. Self-worth would just be a game that those inanimate particles are playing on us. If we are just evolved and not created, it is pointless to try to assign value to ourselves or to anything else because everything is just a random, indiscriminate interaction of molecules, atoms, sub-atomic particles, and energy. Yet evolutionists are faced with a dilemma, because even they feel that sense of significance, but they know it cannot be derived even from a complex arrangement of impersonal atoms plus energy. Where does this universal feeling come from?

The answer to that question should not surprise anyone – creation. We have worth because we are created by an intelligent, personal, omnipotent, omniscient God. He created our first grandparents, Adam and Eve, and He developed each of us in our mothers' wombs. He engineered all my days and He oversees everything about my life.

There are only two options regarding our significance:

1) We are the result of natural selection, the product of the interaction of matter and energy over countless eons. Therefore, our sense of worth is self-generated and is not given to us by anything or anyone outside ourselves. We have no real, ultimate significance.

2) We are a creation of God, made in His image. Therefore, our sense of worth has its origin in the Creator and His purposes for us. We have very real meaning, worth, and eternal significance.

Those are the only two viable options.

RESPOND TO IT

1. Agree/Disagree: If we are not created, our sense of worth is an illusion.

2. Do you agree that the two options discussed at the end of the study are the "only two viable options?"

3

IMPLICATIONS

Goodness

*Creation matters because it explains the
existence of goodness.*

My high school English teacher would not allow us to use the
word "good" in any of our essays. She lectured us that the word
is entirely subjective and that there is no such thing as actual
objective goodness. Ironically she was quite certain that she had
made a very good point. Down deep, I think she knew what we
all know – goodness does exist. Not subjective goodness that is
defined merely by our own preferences and experiences. Not
goodness mandated by someone in power. But real goodness based
on something higher than ourselves. Goodness does not come from
politics, rulers and governments, nor does it come from society
or from self. Because we are created, there is actual, objective,
outside-our-own-selves goodness that originates in the Creator.
It is His goodness that marks all creation. It is His goodness that
our inner compasses point toward. We have a sense of goodness
because that is how the Creator wired us.

Goodness is a common word in Scripture as well as in our
everyday speech. In the Bible it is used to refer to physical beauty,
moral rightness, and inherent value or worth. In the current age, all
of these definitions might be relativized, but in the Bible, they all
exist as objective realities.

An accidental life form called a human can have only an accidental
goodness. In such a scenario, goodness is arbitrary, as it was for
my English teacher. That is the only possibility for the secular
unbeliever. That person can formulate his or her own notions

of goodness, but must recognize that they are based on nothing, apart from personal preferences and/or practical aspirations. Such goodness could change without warning due to fluctuations in our circumstances, health, abilities, or body chemistry.

But if we know that we are created by a good Creator, we are on the path to understanding goodness. We can start understanding goodness by observing creation. Creation is consistent with goodness and reinforces it, but we cannot know what goodness is by merely relying on our own powers of observation and reason. We need revelation. For example, we can look at water, sunshine, babies, fruit trees, and seasons, and deduce that these are good things and that their source is a good Creator. However, unless that Creator has broken through the sound-barrier and communicated to us, we are unable to know much about Him or that those things are actually good.

Of course, Christians and believing Jews have affirmed for thousands of years that the Creator has spoken to us in human language, telling us about Himself and goodness. Because of that, we know that goodness is neither speculative, nor imagined, nor subjective, nor notional, nor emotional. It is objective, knowable, and woven into the fabric of all creation. The fallen-ness of humans and creation does not nullify or obscure goodness, it only clouds and perverts it. It also shows a contrast – When we focus on goodness, it proves our fallen-ness, and when we focus on fallen-ness, it proves the existence of goodness, as reflected in the words of a song by a group called Switchfoot, "The shadow proves the sunshine."

RESPOND TO IT

1. What is goodness?
2. Can people be good without God?
3. Why does creation matter to our understanding of goodness?

4
IMPLICATIONS
Awesome

Creation matters because it shows us that there is Someone outside ourselves.

Throughout this book I will talk about God's glory and our glorifying Him. Most of us have vague, semi-accurate ideas about what these words mean. So it is important that we try to bring some clarity to this topic as we proceed through these studies. It is easier to illustrate than to define the terms. For example, suppose you want to glorify a star athlete. How would you do that? In several ways – You would talk about him often. You would cheer for him with others in the grandstands. You would go to places where he is speaking. You would have pictures of him in your home. You might sing songs about him. You would be drawn to likeminded people who also wish to glorify him. You would read books and articles about him, and be up-to-date on his statistics. If you meet him, you would tell him how great you think he is and how he has impacted your life. You might try to imitate his athletic abilities as well as his off-the-field lifestyle. In short, he would be a model for you, a unifying center of your life, and you would hope that others would also view him the same way. That is an earthly glimpse of what it means to glorify God.

Similarly, what does God's glory mean? Glory is far more than beauty and radiant light, although those are included in it. Imagine that you live in a country ruled by a queen, and that you are watching a parade honoring her for bringing peace and prosperity to the country. She has exercised political, military, and financial power, and she has done it with wisdom and justice for the sake of her people. Even though she is the queen, she has a reputation for being approachable by ordinary people. In the parade she is wearing her royal garments and her crown, and floodlights shine on her and her entourage, and she looks majestic. Her mere presence inspires awe. Here, again, is just an earthly glimpse of what God's glory is.

Non-Christians see the awesome magnificence of creation and give glory to Mother Nature or the cosmos or evolution or natural processes or perhaps something else. They feel compelled to worship something because of what they observe, but since they reject the idea of a Creator, they invent something else to glorify. They worship creation, or something within creation, rather than the true Creator.

Christians, on the other hand, see the awesome magnificence of creation and glorify the Creator. They know that nothing that exists just happened to appear. Everything reflects the power, glory, genius, and personhood of the Creator. There is a God who is external to creation and who is nonetheless manifested and revealed in His creation. The glory we see in creation is real, it is not just something imagined, and that glory is God's glory.

Psalm 19:1 says, "The heavens are telling the glory of God." The heavens are telling us something. For the unbeliever, that "something" is just the glory of impersonal, random forces. For the believer, that "something" is the glory of God. Everyone, believer and unbeliever alike, has an inner impulse to worship either the Creator or something else when they observe the magnificence of creation.

RESPOND TO IT

1. Agree/Disagree: Since everyone worships something, we cannot genuinely worship the one true God unless we believe that He is the Creator.

2. Can you add more examples of what glory means and what it means to glorify someone?

5
IMPLICATIONS
PROBABILITY

Creation matters because it shows us that we are not here by chance.

In responding to the argument that the existence of the heavens and the earth is just random, Christians sometimes argue that the probability of the known universe and a life-sustaining earth coming into existence randomly is so small as to be virtually zero. But that line of reasoning has little effect on the secularist who would respond that huge numbers of events have a nearly 0% probability of happening, but they happen anyway.

We need to be careful in using the probability argument, because probability alone can neither prove nor disprove any event, including creation. However, probability does tell us something. If not proving creation, it at least points to it as being possible. We ought not to ignore probability as we examine sequences and/or combinations of events. In the case of the heavens and the earth, probability makes belief in creation reasonable.

For example, in a court of law, a defendant is presumed innocent until proven guilty. So, the attorneys build a case based on evidence and the probability of each piece of evidence. In a well investigated case, at a certain point, that combined probability enables the jury to reach a verdict. We can apply this approach to the topic of creation. Namely, at a certain point, when all of the probabilities related to life, the earth, and the universe are considered, we can say that it is reasonable to conclude that this is all more than the result of purely natural processes and that it is the creation by a powerful divine Being, specifically the God of the Bible. The probability of the known universe with all its intricacies, complexities and inter-dependencies coming into being through unguided natural causes is so small that it would require at least as much faith to believe that as to believe in the Creator-God.

Each particular piece of creation can be assigned a measurable, even if very low, probability of occurring through natural processes, such as the earth orbiting the sun in a zone conducive to life, the human reproductive process, or the existence of organs such as lungs, the digestive track, and the eye, and the complex interaction of complex bodily systems. But when thousands of such events are strung together or overlaid on top of each other, their collective probability is so low that we should take notice. This may not prove creation, but it gives credible evidence for it.

The point is this: As we explore our complex universe and world, eventually we come to a point where we can reasonably say that the probability of creation happening by natural causes is for all intents and purposes 0%, but the probability of it coming into existence by a divine Creator for all intents-and-purposes is 100%. While secularists may turn a blind eye and look for naturalistic explanations, Christians on the other hand, drop to their knees in awe of the One who is not bound by probabilities but whose glory, wisdom, and power are revealed in creation.

RESPOND TO IT

1. Agree/Disagree: Probability alone cannot prove or disprove creation.

2. What role does probability play in your thinking about creation?

6
IMPLICATIONS
REALITY

*Creation matters because it is why we believe
in objective reality.*

Descartes famously said: "I think, therefore I am." Most of us would have said: "I am, therefore I think." Actually, Descartes should have said, "I am created, therefore I both am and think." Descartes and others have been bothered by the philosophical question of whether or not we actually exist. Most of us do not worry about that; it seems fairly obvious to the normal person on his or her way to work each morning. Based on Scripture, the Christian confidently asserts that our existence and objective reality are not illusions. Space, time and human beings are realities because they are created.

We do not live in an illusionary world. We have self-consciousness because we are whole human beings made in the image of a self-conscious God. Each of us is separate from all other people, animals, and other created things. All humans are like each other because we are all bearers of the image of God, but we are also individually unique beings. We exist in objective reality, and we are not imagining the universe around us; it is really there as are all people and creatures that reside in it.

Our world and universe are not eternally permanent, but they are fixed because the Creator is unchanging. This is one of many ways that creation reflects attributes of our Creator. The world is not morphing into ever-changing realities like the oil in "Lava lamps" from the 1970's. There is a consistent, solid objective reality that we humans can explore, discover, and analyze. That reality will still be there tomorrow.

Because the Creator is unchanging, His creation, humans included, remains what it was originally created to be. The laws of physics and mathematics yesterday are still the same today. We may know more about them, and we may be making new discoveries, but those fixed laws do not change. Jeremiah said as much in 33:25 when he compared God's loyalty to His people to the permanence of the fixed laws of nature: *"But this is what the LORD says: I would no more reject my people than I would change my laws that govern night and day, earth and sky."* (New Living Translation) Scientists can do research because physical phenomena are repeatable and the laws that govern them are consistent.

We explore and discover reality, but we do not and cannot create it. There are significant implications to this. For one, all scientific inquiry depends on the objective nature of creation, because reality exists in and of itself, and is not dependent upon the observer. For another, if the physical world with its laws and axioms is objective, then likewise, so may be the immaterial world. The Christian accepts the idea that there are both physical realities and spiritual realities that do not depend on human invention or verification because the Bible clearly tells us that both of those realities are there, independent of us.

We are not living in an illusion, despite Albert Einstein's assertion: "Reality is merely an illusion, albeit a very persistent one." Just because one of the world's most brilliant men said something, it is not necessarily true. It's too bad Einstein did not think through that conclusion as carefully and thoroughly as he did his theories about physics and math. He might have concluded that we have a persistent illusion of reality precisely because there actually is reality. Also, it might have helped him to have contemplated the biblical perspective on the topic – "In the beginning God created the heavens and the earth." Reality does not start with us, but with God. God is, therefore we are.

RESPOND TO IT

1. In this study we have noted a couple definitions and metaphors for reality. Complete one or both of the following sentences:

Reality is _____ .

Reality is like _____ .

7
IMPLICATIONS
REASON AND TRUTH

Creation matters because it explains the existence of truth and our ability to know it.

While some people are not reasonable much of the time, and all of us are unreasonable some of the time, no one is unreasonable all of the time. The reason is: No one is without reason. We are all born with it. It is not soley a matter of intelligence or education. Without reason, we would not be able to learn, converse, decide, or plan. We live in a culture where reason is often supplanted by experience and where truth is relativized. But, for that to happen, there must first be reason and truth.

Widespread rejection of God is leading to a dreadful inversion of truth and right thinking. Romans 1:18-32 summarizes that better than any writing since the first century. While this is a lengthy passage, it is important for us to read it carefully as we proceed with this topic.

Romans 1:18-32

18 For the wrath of God is revealed from heaven against all ungodliness and unrighteousness of men who suppress the truth in unrighteousness, 19 because that which is known about God is evident within them; for God made it evident to them. 20 For since the creation of the world His invisible attributes, His eternal power and divine nature, have been clearly seen, being understood through what has been made, so that they are without excuse. 21 For even though they knew God, they did not honor Him as God or give thanks, but they became futile in their speculations, and their foolish heart was darkened. 22 *Professing to be wise, they became fools, 23 and exchanged the glory of the incorruptible God for an image in the form of corruptible man and of birds and four-footed animals and crawling creatures. 24 Therefore God gave them over in the lusts of their hearts to impurity, so that their bodies would be dishonored among them. 25 For they exchanged the truth of God for a lie, and worshiped and served the creature rather than the Creator, who is blessed forever. Amen. 26 For this reason God gave them over to degrading passions; for their women exchanged the natural function for that which is unnatural, 27 and in the same way also the men abandoned the natural function of the woman and burned in their desire toward one another, men with men committing indecent acts and receiving in their own persons the due penalty of their error.*

28 *And just as they did not see fit to acknowledge God any longer, God gave them over to a depraved mind, to do those things which are not proper, 29 being filled with all unrighteousness, wickedness, greed, evil; full of envy, murder, strife, deceit, malice; they are gossips, 30 slanderers, haters of God, insolent, arrogant, boastful, inventors of evil, disobedient to parents, 31 without understanding, untrustworthy, unloving, unmerciful; 32 and although they know the ordinance of God, that those who practice such things are worthy of death, they not only do the same, but also give hearty approval to those who practice them.*

The climactic verse in the passage is verse 28, and two words are crucial, "depraved mind." They mean something more than just warped thinking, evil motives, and criminal intentions. If that is all the words mean, they should occur at the beginning of the passage, but Paul uses them near the end, saving them to describe something worse than what he has already discussed in the preceding verses. They describe where people and societies end up after going through the stages of rebellion against God that were outlined in verses 21-27. These two words actually are saying that the rejection of God leads not only initially to moral perversion, but eventually to something far more sinister – depraved minds. In other words, depraved minds do not cause atheism and moral deviancy, they result from it. By definition, depraved minds are minds that invert right and wrong, truth and falsehood, good and evil. At this stage, people no longer are choosing to violate what is right, or to lie against the truth, or to choose what is not good. Rather at this stage they are reversing definitions, so that wrong is now called "right," deception is called "truth," and evil is seen as "good." The evidences of this flip-flopped thinking are described in verses 29-31. They proclaim that we should not just tolerate those inversions, but that we should celebrate them, as verse 32 concludes.

The Romans passage shows the regression that occurs when people start rejecting the basic truth about God that is apparent to every person. It leads to a wholesale rejection of God, truth, and right thinking, unless a person is converted by God's grace to Jesus Christ. Because God is a God of truth, He designed us, in His image, to also know and rely on truth. Non-Christians can and should acknowledge that, but Romans 1 and our own experience confirm that they often do not. Christians are under obligation to acknowledge it.

Despite many people's protestations, everyone believes in truth, at least as they begin their lives. The disagreements come over defining truth and determining the limits of our reason. Even the post-modern relativist believes that his or her denial of truth is, in fact, truthful. Of course, hardly anyone believes that there is nothing that is true. Even most relativists still believe that there is mathematical truth, scientific truth, and circumstantial truth.

If reason and truth exist, where did they come from? How do we explain the universal affirmation of reason and truth in every human being? It's almost as if something or Someone put them into us. And that is precisely the point. Someone did.

The weather changes, opinions change, and health changes, but the fact that those "truths" may change from day to day does not mean that all truth is equally changeable. There are enduring truths upon which we all rely. For example, at a most basic level, we know that 7 x 3 will always be 21 and gravity will always hold us to the surface of the earth. We know that every person will eventually die. Those facts are unchanging and true, and they will not go away if we ignore or deny them. We rely on such truths and base many enduring concepts, fields of study, and our own creations on them, such as architecture, medicine, and aerospace programs. We have the ability to observe and understand them through our reason, and most people do not even wonder why these things are so because it all seems so natural and logical.

The explanation for reason and truth being universal, natural and logical is that there is a God who created us and He is reasonable and truthful. He made us in His image, and He built reason and truth into our souls. In Isaiah 1:18, God says, "Come now, let us reason together..." He could say that because He made us as reasonable creatures. We can reason because God reasons.

Through our reason we can discover and deduce many truths. But some truths are beyond our natural reason, and we receive them by revelation from God in the pages of the Bible. In each of these scenarios, rather than creating truth, we are discovering it. Truth exists outside us, and is not generated from within us. It is not dependent upon the observer.

Actual truth is not slippery and changing, but conclusions that we draw from truth may be. Like the woman who told the man she was breaking up with: "I'll always treasure my original misperception of you." Or, like when people say: "I have my truth and you have yours." They are really saying, "I have my opinions and you have yours." But peeling that thinking back just a little, we come to the simple fact that each of us bases our opinions on observable truths outside ourselves, truths that we interpret and turn into opinions. At some layer beneath our opinions lies a bedrock of truth, which is neither mine nor yours, but everyone's.

In his song "Sweet Surrender," John Denver missed the point when he sang: "There's nothing that binds me to something that might have been true yesterday." He was reflecting a contemporary view that truth is ever-changing, which ironically is itself an unchanging assertion of truth. He saw only that the circumstances in his life were changing, but he failed to recognize that the truths underlying those circumstances were unchanging. That is, there are certain things that were true about his life and about the world, even if he did not realize it.

We can behave in ways that violate relational truths and cause problems, but the truths remain unchanged. We can deny right and wrong, causing pain for ourselves and others, but the right and wrong are not changed. We can ignore or reject spiritual realities, but they do not cease to exist because we do so, nor do they morph if we decide to change our views of God. The working out of truth may change, but the actual truth does not. Truth exists because God exists, and He wove it into His creation.

RESPOND TO IT

1. Regarding reason, truth, facts, and opinions, what does change, and what does not?

2. Reread Romans 1:18-32 and discuss how it summarizes the results of rejecting God.

   What evidences of this do you see in our culture?

3. There are Christians who are skeptical of human reason, saying that we should just rely on God's revelation in Scripture. Are you one of them? Why or why not?

4. What is the balance between reason and faith?

8
IMPLICATIONS
CONTEXT

Creation matters because it is the framework in which we can contextualize what is happening.

Acts 4:24-30

24And when they heard this, they lifted their voices to God with one accord and said, "O Lord, it is You who MADE THE HEAVEN AND THE EARTH AND THE SEA, AND ALL THAT IS IN THEM, 25who by the Holy Spirit, through the mouth of our father David Your servant, said, 'Why did the Gentiles rage, And the peoples devise futile things? 26'The kings of the earth took their stand, And the rulers were gathered together Against the Lord and against His Christ.' 27For truly in this city there were gathered together against Your holy servant Jesus, whom You anointed, both Herod and Pontius Pilate, along with the Gentiles and the peoples of Israel, 28to do whatever Your hand and Your purpose predestined to occur. 29And now, Lord, take note of their threats, and grant that Your bond-servants may speak Your word with all confidence, 30while You extend Your hand to heal, and signs and wonders take place through the name of Your holy servant Jesus."

When the first persecution against the apostles occurred, notice how they began their prayer. We might have expected them to start with some kind of reference to God's power, justice, and/or protection, but they went straight to creation. They were doing more than following the A-C-T-S model – Adoration-Confession-Thanksgiving-Supplication. That is a very good model for prayer, but it is not the only model. It is not like the apostles said to themselves, "OK, for the Adoration part of our prayer today, let's mention that God created everything, and then we can get into the real reason for our prayer."

In the face of imminent danger, opposition, and persecution, we might have expected them to recall God's past deliverances and that He is a fortress and protector for His people. Rather, their first thought in the face of developing persecution was that God is the Creator. They knew that they were praying to the One who made everything, even their persecutors, and that He was not an impersonal force, a mercenary god, or an on-demand deity. They were asking the Creator of all to intervene in His creation to make things right with His created people.

In light of knowing that God created everything in heaven and earth, we, like the apostles, can face current events. If this world is His creation and humans were made by Him, then it makes sense that current events are the outworking of His purposes, as Acts 4:28 asserts: *"to do whatever Your hand and Your purpose predestined to occur."*

If God did not create everything, current events are random and purposeless, and we have no hope for anything better. There would be no point in praying because these events would simply be the way that things happen in a naturalistic, materialistic world. If this is not God's creation, we reside in an uncertain place. If there is a god, but one who did not create the universe, maybe this non-creator god can do something about events, or maybe not. We would have no assurance that he has the power to have any effect on our lives.

But if this is God's creation, we can pray confidently, knowing that He is working out His purposes. He oversaw the events of Christ's arrest and execution (Acts 4:27), He spoke to His creation (Acts 4:25), He is undaunted by opposition (Acts 4:25-26), He overrides the laws of nature to accomplish His purposes (Acts 4:30), and He controls the speech of His servants (Acts 4:29). He is still overseeing events today in exactly those same ways.

The early apostles' prayer in Acts 4:24-30 assures us that God is the Creator of everything and that the things that happen in our lives are according to His purposes, and that He is in control. He is overseeing even the hostile forces against us; they are not alien to Him; He made them. He is not confined by or troubled by the laws of nature or by the behavior of our adversaries, but He can and does intervene at will. He is never surprised, never perplexed, and never worried. Because He is the Creator, we can relax. When we pray at the times of trouble, we should remember how the apostles prayed when they faced persecution, and start with acknowledging that everything that exists is His creation. If creation was hugely important to the early apostles, why do we hardly think of it? Why do we rarely begin our prayers as the apostles did in Acts 4:24? We should. It puts everything into perspective.

If He created everything, He can handle this.

RESPOND TO IT

1. How do you begin your prayers? How frequently do you mention creation when you pray? Why did the apostles begin their prayer with a reference to creation?

2. Discuss: "If creation was hugely important to the early apostles, why do we hardly think of it? Why do we rarely begin our prayers as the apostles did in Acts 4:24?"

3. "Because He is the Creator, we can relax." That sounds nice in a Bible study, but how can we actually work that out when things are not going well?

9

IMPLICATIONS
HUMANITY'S PARENTS

*Creation matters because it explains who
our first parents were.*

For the Darwinist, Adam and Eve are irrelevant, except as characters out of religious mythology. But, for the Christian, Adam and Eve are central to our understanding of who we are as human beings. According to the Bible, they:

- were a literal man and woman

- had no parents, but were a unique creation of God – Adam from the dust of the ground, Eve from Adam's rib

- existed in a specific time and place in history

- were the original parents of all humans

- brought sin into the human race, contaminating the whole world with it

- passed on to their descendants both their genetic code and their predisposition to sin

- were the prototype humans, made in the image of God

- were a different species and kind from all other life forms

- were the first ancestors of mankind's Redeemer

- are the explanation for the condition of mankind to this day

Prior to them there is no recorded human history. Beginning with them we have detailed recorded history. The whole Bible affirms the literal historicity of Adam and Eve.

- Genealogies are traced back to them. Genealogies cannot be traced to legends, fictitious people, figurative characters, or mythical individuals. For example, no one can claim to be a descendant of Huckleberry Finn. Adam and Eve were not just symbolic representations of humankind or the culmination of a long family line. They were physical, flesh-and-blood people with a genetic code unrelated to any other being. They were brand new when they appeared, and the whole human race traces back to them. The entire human population in the world today is attributable to Adam and Eve.

- Jesus referred to them as actual individuals (Matthew 19:4).

- Paul compared the literal Jesus to the literal Adam (1 Corinthians 15:22, 45)

- Paul used the actual Adam and Eve as the basis for his teaching about the identity and roles of the genders (1 Timothy 2:13-14).

Adam and Eve were real people in recorded history, and we are all their grandchildren.

RESPOND TO IT

1. How do the points in this study impact your view of people who are different from you? similar to you?

2. Because everyone's genealogy goes back to Adam and Eve, there is only one race – the human race. Discuss the implications of this.

10

IMPLICATIONS
INFINITE VS. FINITE

*Creation matters because it keeps our views
of God and us in perspective.*

Creation tells us many things about God, one of which is that He existed, necessarily, before creation. *"Even from everlasting to everlasting, You are God,"* Psalm 90:2. He had no beginning or end, and there is no limit to His size. He always was. He always will be. He is everywhere.

Nothing created can be greater than its creator. So, logically, God is larger than the created universe...infinitely so. God is undaunted by the enormity of the universe because He made it. He is both external to it and involved in it. So, we cannot go anywhere within it or outside it and get away from its Creator.

God is infinite in both space and time. We are finite in both space and time. God is also infinite in His knowledge, but our knowledge is partial. As amazing as the human brain is, it still has a limit as to how much it can know. Our physical bodies assure us that our knowledge will always be finite.

We can understand that there is knowledge outside our ability to know, knowledge possessed by the Creator but unavailable to us or beyond our comprehension. We are created in God's image, so we have the capacity to know things, especially things required to sustain life and to know God. But just as the universe is not infinite, neither is our knowledge.

Creation also shows us God's infinite power. We can observe

unfathomable power in the universe, from phenomena in interstellar space to the explosive power of sub-atomic particles. No power can be self-generated, only derived from a higher power. There is no power outside God's design, creation and control. His power is necessarily greater than all other powers. Our power is limited. We have influence on some aspects of creation, but all it takes is an earthquake, a hurricane, a tsunami, a plague, a forest fire, or a tornado for us to see how small and finite our power is compared to God's.

God is bigger than creation, older than creation, more powerful than creation, more knowledgeable than creation, and more long-lasting than creation. He is independent of creation; He is dependent on nothing. But we are created beings, dependent on Him and the created world on which He has placed us. We depend on His power, knowledge, presence and eternality. The fact that He is infinite and eternal puts our lives into perspective, and assures us that everything is under control.

RESPOND TO IT

1. How is God's infinite-ness and our finite-ness both humbling and reassuring?

2. How would you describe God's infinite-ness to a 7-year-old child?

THE CREATOR

The main point of creation is the Creator. Unless we are drawn to Him in awe and humility, we have missed the whole point of studying the biblical teaching about creation. Studies 11-28 direct our attention to who God is in light of many passages that refer to Him as the Creator.

Most of us, when we see the word "God" in Scripture, automatically assume that it is referring to God the Father. But in actuality, much of the time it is referring to the triune God – Father, Son, and Holy Spirit. Such is the case when we look at the doctrine of creation. There are hundreds of verses that say that God created the heavens and the earth, yet only a handful specifically mentions the Father. Another handful mentions the Son. And yet another handful mentions the Holy Spirit. The point is this: When we read in the Old and New Testaments that God is the Creator, we need to realize that it is the triune God who did the creating.

11
THE CREATOR
THE TRINITY

Creation matters because it introduces us to the one God who has existed as a Trinity from eternity.

From eternity to eternity God has existed and will exist as one God in three persons. When Genesis 1:1 says, "In the beginning God created the heavens and the earth," it is telling us that "God the Father, Son and Holy Spirit created the heavens and the earth." Everything visible and invisible was created by the triune God, not just one member of the Trinity.

Genesis 1:26 introduces us to this triune Creator: "Then God said, 'Let Us make man in Our image, according to Our likeness.'" The plural pronouns are noteworthy. Godly Bible scholars who believe in biblical inerrancy have explained this in different ways. Some would say that angels are included in the plural pronouns. But we are made in God's image, not in angels' image. Also, there is no mention of angels in Genesis 1, so it is a huge interpretive stretch to see angels as included in the plural pronouns. The interpretation that makes most sense to me is the one that sees these plural pronouns as a reference to the plurality within the Godhead – Father, Son and Holy Spirit. Humans are made in the likeness of the triune God. We are image-bearers not of the Father alone, but of the Father, Son, and Holy Spirit.

This view is consistent with the Hebrew word for God in Genesis 1, *Elohim*, which is a masculine plural word. That He is both plural yet one God is affirmed by the words in the context of Genesis 1, specifically the singular verbs, such as "said," verse 26, and other singular pronouns, such as "His own image," verse 27. To summarize, the language of Genesis 1 introduces us to the Creator who is simultaneously both one and plural, which is exactly what the historic doctrine of the Trinity affirms, namely one God in three Persons.

CREATION – WORK OF GOD THE FATHER

1 Corinthians 8:6

Yet for us there is but one God, the Father, from whom are all things and we exist for Him; and one Lord, Jesus Christ, by whom are all things, and we exist through Him.

Malachi 2:10

Do we not all have one father? Has not one God created us?

Isaiah 64:8

But now, O Lord, You are our Father,
We are the clay, and You our potter;
And all of us are the work of Your hand.

"We believe in one God, the Father, the Almighty, maker of heaven and earth, of all that is, seen and unseen." (Nicene Creed)

The biblical affirmation is clear: creation is the work of God the Father, not in isolation from the Son and the Holy Spirit, but in perfect unity with them. All things are "from" Him, and therefore our purpose as human beings is "for" Him, namely to acknowledge Him as God and glorify Him. He is our originator, our Creator. He is the "Father of all things" similar to the way that George Washington was the "Father of our country," only on a much grander scale. He is the only explanation for our existence.

This leads us into the work of God the Son, which has already been mentioned in 1 Corinthians 8:6.

CREATION – WORK OF GOD THE SON

John 1:1-4, 10-11

1In the beginning was the Word, and the Word was with God, and the Word was God. 2He was in the beginning with God. 3All things came into being through Him, and apart from Him nothing came into being that has come into being. 4In Him was life, and the life was the Light of men ...

10He was in the world, and the world was made through Him, and the world did not know Him. 11He came to His own, and those who were His own did not receive Him.

Colossians 1:15-17

15He is the image of the invisible God, the firstborn of all creation. 16For by Him all things were created, both in the heavens and on earth, visible and invisible, whether thrones or dominions or rulers or authorities—all things have been created through Him and for Him. 17He is before all things, and in Him all things hold together.

Hebrews 1:1-3, 8, 10

1God, after He spoke long ago to the fathers in the prophets in many portions and in many ways, 2 in these last days has spoken to us in His Son, whom He appointed heir of all things, through whom also He made the world.3And He is the radiance of His glory and the exact representation of His nature, and upholds all things by the word of His power...

10And [of the Son He says], "You, Lord, in the beginning laid the foundation of the earth, And the heavens are the works of Your hands.

A few years ago I was teaching an adult class at my church, and one of the ladies said to me, "All we do in this Sunday School class is talk about Jesus. I'd like to ask that we do a study about God."

Besides being borderline heretical, her comment encapsulated what I think is a prevailing idea among modern Christians, namely that there is God the Father who is really God, then there is the Son of God, Jesus Christ, who is somewhat lesser, and finally there is the Holy Spirit, tagging along in third place. We know we should believe that they are all somehow equally God, but it just seems that the Father is more equal than the other two. People seem to think of the Trinity as a three-tiered deity, with the Father being the top tier, and Jesus being tier-two, and the Holy Spirit occupying the tier-three position. In reality, all three are equally tier-one God.

The verses cited above tell us several important things about the Creator God. One in particular is that Jesus Christ is not only the revelation of God to human beings; He is also God the Son who had a prominent role in the creation of human beings and the universe in which we reside. The entirety of creation is the work of the pre-incarnate Jesus Christ. The implications are enormous.

Implication #1: To deny the doctrine of creation is to disbelieve what the Bible says about Christ. To put it another way: It is not possible to claim to believe in Jesus but also to not believe in creation. According to the Scriptures, Jesus created, owns, sustains, and rules over everything. If we deny, or even doubt, that Jesus is the Creator, we will have a hard time really believing that He is Lord and that He owns and sustains the earth and life on it. If He is not the Creator, He is just an appointee, charged with overseeing someone else's possession. However, since He is the Creator, this is a world that is permeated by Him and bears His fingerprints. But we will be blind to that if we do not realize that Jesus is the God who made everything that exists. If we do not trust in Christ as Creator, we cannot fully trust in Him as Lord.

Implication #2: Jesus has first place with reference to all creation. Therefore, He alone should be worshiped. If we adore anything else above Him, that thing or person is an idol.

Implication #3: Jesus' creative work was not partial, nor did He merely initiate creation, nor was He simply an on-site supervisor of the creation project. The totality of the existing known universe was created by Him. That includes all natural laws and processes, none of which have ever operated independently of Him. Everything we discover about our world and universe was created by Jesus Christ. Every natural law was His design; all atomic particles and structures were made by Him; all life was His creation; everything in the skies above was put there by Him. He holds it all together — *"He is before all things, and in Him all things hold together,"* Colossians 1:17. Therefore, every scientific discovery should remind us that Jesus Christ is the Designer, Creator, and Sustainer.

Implication #4: Jesus is the visible expression of the invisible God. He not only made this world, but He entered it in history as a man to reveal the triune God to us. God has spoken to us through Jesus Christ, and in Him we see the Father. Christ made this planet, visited this planet, and still resides on this planet through His Holy Spirit. No one can know God apart from Christ; He and the Father are one. None of us can know God directly without a mediator, and that is Jesus.

CREATION – WORK OF GOD THE HOLY SPIRIT

Genesis 1:1-2

1In the beginning God created the heavens and the earth. 2The earth was formless and void, and darkness was over the surface of the deep, and the Spirit of God was moving over the surface of the waters.

Job 33:4

"The Spirit of God has made me,
And the breath of the Almighty gives me life.

Psalm 33:6

6By the word of the LORD the heavens were made,
And by the breath of His mouth all their host.

Psalm 104:30

You send forth Your Spirit, they are created;
And You renew the face of the ground.

If you were reading the Old Testament in the original Hebrew, you would not find separate words for "spirit" and "breath." Rather, you would find a single Hebrew word, *ruach*, which is translated "spirit" sometimes and "breath" other times, as well as "wind" in several verses. You would need to consider the immediate context to determine which meaning was intended, but even then it would not always be clear. In some cases, such as Psalm 33:6 referenced above, it seems that the author deliberately intended for the reader to understand "breath," *ruach*, as a juxtaposition of both meanings – God's Spirit and God's breath.

Another Hebrew word for "breath," *neshamah*, is occasionally used in the Old Testament. It is the word that we find in the second half of Job 33:4. The verse is a form of Hebrew poetry called "synonymous parallelism" in which the second part is synonymous with the first part. Hence, we see that *ruach*, translated "Spirit" in the first part, is synonymous with *neshamah*. We see this same parallelism in the prose of Genesis 2:7 and 6:17. Both verses contain the phrase "the breath of life." In Genesis 2:7 the Hebrew word is *neshamah* but in Genesis 6:17 the word is *ruach*. The point of these brief word studies is to point out that the Scriptures affirm that life itself is the work of God the Holy Spirit (*ruach*).

CONCLUSION

There is one, and only one, Creator God. He is a God who has existed eternally in three co-equal persons – Father, Son, and Holy Spirit. Each is a co-agent of creation. When we read the hundreds of verses that talk about God or the Lord being the Creator of the heavens and the earth, we can safely understand that the triune God is that Creator. In a handful of verses, as we have seen, we are informed that the individual persons of the Godhead were involved in creation, but they were so united in their creative work that we cannot separate their roles in the process as if they had separate job descriptions.

Throughout this book, when I talk about the Creator God, I specifically mean the triune God, because that is the only God who is there.

RESPOND TO IT

1. When we say that God created the heavens and earth, we are actually saying that God the Father, God the Son (Jesus Christ), and God the Holy Spirit did it. To what extent do you think Christians generally believe that? To what extent do you believe it?

2. What difference does it make to you to understand that we are the creation of the triune God?

3. Do you think of the trinity as a three-tiered God?

4. 4. Agree/Disagree: "If we do not trust in Christ as the Creator, we cannot fully trust in Him is Lord."

12

THE CREATOR
LORD AND GOD

Creation matters because it is the explanation
for God's lordship over the world.

This is God's creation, not someone else's. He is the Lord of something that He created. It's not like He was drifting around space one day and came across the universe and decided to take charge. This is His world in His universe, and everything in them is His. When the Bible says that He is the Lord, one of the things it means is that He is in control. A person who builds a business from scratch is in control of that business. God built the universe from scratch and He controls –

- the way atoms work

- weather patterns

- seasons

- physics, chemistry, biology, astronomy, geology, ecology

- mathematics

- reproduction

- gravity

Despite knowing better, we have a tendency to think of the heavens and earth as somehow independent of God. Oh, we know that He is God and that He reigns over heaven and earth. Yet, in everyday ways we have difficulty seeing the things of this world as falling under His administration, things like medicine, politics, technology, global weather, social issues, the economy, and so forth. Add to that list things like wars, terrorism, crime, civil unrest, droughts, natural calamities, and epidemics, and we wonder how much He really controls, and we start to think that maybe this is not really My Father's world. We pray occasionally about such things and say we believe that God is powerful and majestic, but... and that is precisely where we go off the rails. As soon as we say "but" we are showing our doubt about God's actual lordship over all of creation. In this regard we are practical agnostics.

It is like we think that there are earth rules, and then there are God's rules, and maybe they overlap a little but certainly not entirely. In other words, many of us believe that the earth is governed by the laws of science, and our spiritual and moral lives are governed by God, and the two generally keep their distance from each other. Consequently we think that we should not bring God into science, and we should keep science away from God; that there is the natural, material, visible world, and then there is the spiritual, invisible world, and we should not try to superimpose either one on the other. We know that non-Christians think like this, if they acknowledge God at all, but unfortunately too many Christians think like this also.

We believers need to come to the point where we truly believe that God actually is the Creator and Lord of this earth and everything in it. We need to resist the idea that He is a benign deity who either lost control or never had it. If we really believe God is Creator and Lord, we have a starting place for understanding the complexities of life on this planet. If we really believe that this actually is God's world, we will be able to see that Scripture provides more insights and answers than we may have thought. The Lord is at work in our lives by His Spirit, pushing us to get past our practical agnosticism to the place where we believe that what the Scriptures say is real.

God did not invade and usurp ownership of someone else's creation. This is His world. He made it. He owns it. He holds it together. He controls it. He visited it physically in the person of Jesus Christ. And through Christ, He is redeeming us, both in and out of this world.

Isaiah 45:7, 8, 12, 18

7The One forming light and creating darkness, Causing well-being and creating calamity; I am the LORD who does all these 8"Drip down, O heavens, from above And let the clouds pour down righteousness Let the earth open up and salvation bear fruit And righteousness spring up with it. I, the LORD, have created it... 12"It is I who made the earth, and created man upon it. I stretched out the heavens with My hands And I ordained all their host... 18For thus says the LORD, who created the heavens (He is the God who formed the earth and made it, He established it and did not create it a waste place, but formed it to be inhabited), "I am the LORD, and there is none else.

RESPOND TO IT

1. Most Christians know that the Bible teaches that God is in control of His creation. In our daily lives, when we watch the news, and when we observe what is happening around us, to what extent do we actually – mentally and emotionally – believe this?

2. How would things be different in our lives if we believed this more fully?

3. To what extent are we "practical agnostics?"

13
THE CREATOR
A GLIMPSE

*Creation matters because it gives us a glimpse
of the God who designed and rules over the
heavens and earth and their natural laws.*

Long before modern science or even the invention of the telescope, God's Word told us some fundamental things about earth science. The book of Job is considered to be the oldest book in the Bible, predating the books of Moses. Even Job understood several basic facts about the earth. (Some of these will be discussed in more detail in later sections.)

First, in Job 26:7, Job said *"He stretches out the north over empty space, And hangs the earth on nothing."* He knew that the earth exists in space with no supporting structure or physical foundation. It hangs on nothing, in space, governed by invisible laws of astrophysics. And God did that. The lesson learned is that God established the laws of physics; He designed the way the solar system works.

Three verses later, in Job 26:10, Job acknowledged that the earth is round, *"He has inscribed a circle on the surface of the waters, At the boundary of light and darkness."* From the earliest times, people have observed the curvature of the earth as they looked at the horizon. The easiest place to see that was standing on a shore looking out over the sea. Job knew that the earth was circular, and by implication spherical. No Bible-believer should ever have conjectured that the earth is flat. It is a round sphere hanging in space on nothing except for the invisible forces that God put in place.

Because God made the world, He also designed and controls

geophysics and astrophysics. He created and controls:

- the weather – Job 26:8-9: 8 *"He wraps up the waters in His clouds, And the cloud does not burst under them.* 9 *"He obscures the face of the full moon And spreads His cloud over it."*

- earth's magnetic fields – Job 26:7a: *"He stretches out the north over empty space..."* This idea was picked up later by the Psalmist – Psalm 89:12: *"The north and the south, You have created them."* Job seemed to understand that the earth's magnetic field extended from the north out into space, as scientific research has confirmed.

- light and darkness – Job 26:10: *"He has inscribed a circle on the surface of the waters At the boundary of light and darkness."*

- oceanography – Job 26:12: *"He quieted the sea with His power..."*

- animal life – Job 26:13b: *"His hand has pierced the fleeing serpent."*

Why did Job recite all these things that God controls? Partly to show how powerful He is. Partly to show that we have only a glimpse of who God is. In Job 26:14, he says, *"Behold, these are the fringes of His ways; And how faint a word we hear of Him! But His mighty thunder, who can understand?"* When we see the awesome size, majesty, and power of the universe, we are seeing just a glimpse of its Creator. If we cannot completely understand something as simple as thunder, as Job 26:14 suggests, we should tremble with awe before the God who hangs the earth in space, establishes the laws of science, and controls the weather. We are getting only a glimpse of this great Creator, a true glimpse, but only a glimpse nonetheless.

RESPOND TO IT

1. To what extent do you actually believe that God controls weather, gravity, and astrophysics?

2. Discuss the concluding sentence of this study: "We are getting only a glimpse of this great Creator, a true glimpse, but only a glimpse nonetheless."

14
THE CREATOR
ETERNAL

Creation matters because it defines our place in history.

Psalm 90:2
Before the mountains were born
Or You gave birth to the earth and the world, Even from
everlasting to everlasting, You are God.

Psalm 102:25-26
25 "Of old You founded the earth,
And the heavens are the work of Your hands.
26 "Even they will perish, but You endure;
And all of them will wear out like a garment;
Like clothing You will change them and they will be changed.

In basic Math classes, the number line is a very useful tool for solving many problems. It looks like this:

-∞ ∞

-10 -9 -8 -7 -6 -5 -4 -3 -2 -1 0 +1 +2 +3 +4 +5 +6 +7 +8 +9 +10

The arrows at the ends of the line indicate that the numbers go on to infinity, in both directions. To indicate all the numbers beginning with 5 and ending with 12, we would use interval notation to write [5,12]. To indicate all the numbers greater than 5 and less than 12, we would write (5,12). The square brackets [_,_] indicate that the lower and upper numbers are included in the interval, whereas the curved parentheses (_,_) indicate that the lower and upper numbers are excluded. Negative and positive infinity, ∞ and -∞, would be enclosed with the curved parentheses, because there is no final number that can be identified with infinity.

So what is the point of this brief basic Math lesson? The number line and interval notation illustrate what Psalm 90:2 and 102:25-26 are saying. Specifically:

God:	(-∞, ∞)
Heavens and Earth: [Creation, End]	

Using a number line, we could diagram each scenario like this:

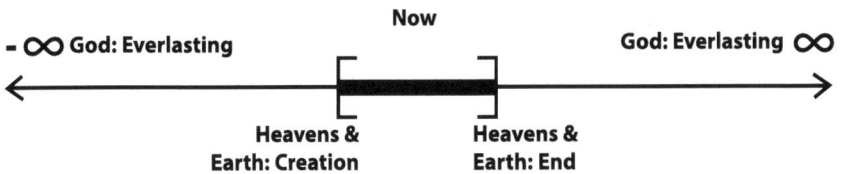

When we look at it this way, we can see a few things.

First, this shows why the psalmist wrote, *"For a thousand years in Your sight are like yesterday when it passes by,"* Psalm 90:4. A thousand years on earth are just a little blip on the time-line compared to the eternality of the Creator. The conclusion of this number line is not mathematical but doxological. That is, as we see the relative brevity of the created universe, we should be awed by the eternal God.

Second, there was a point in real history, before which there was nothing except the triune God, and immediately after which there was a physical universe. And just as things began in a flash, so they will culminate.

2 Peter 3:10

But the day of the Lord will come like a thief, in which the heavens will pass away with a roar and the elements will be destroyed with intense heat, and the earth and its works will be burned up.

That will be followed immediately by a new creation that will last into eternity. There will be a new heavens and a new earth which will be created instantaneously as were the present ones.

2 Peter 3:13

But according to His promise we are looking for new heavens and a new earth, in which righteousness dwells.

Revelation 21:1

Then I saw a new heaven and a new earth; for the first heaven and the first earth passed away, and there is no longer any sea.

Isaiah 66:22

"For just as the new heavens and the new earth Which I make will endure before Me," declares the LORD, "So your offspring and your name will endure."

Even the end of all things and the creation of the new heavens and the new earth are modeled on the original creation of all things.

Third, we need to look to the past to understand who, what, and where we are now. Working backwards in time, the further back we go, the more we rely on the testimonies and records of others.

Within our lifetime – For most people, our memories serve us well. We remember the people and circumstances that shaped our lives. We clearly see how the events of the past five minutes have a direct impact on what we are experiencing now. Similarly, we can see how the events of yesterday, last week, last year and ten years ago also shaped our lives. We can trace our personal history back to our earliest memories, and we do not need to think too hard to understand how it all has led us to where we are right now.

The previous generation – All of us know people, like our parents, who were alive before we were born. By listening to them, we learn what life was like before we showed up. Their stories become our stories, because they explain who our families are, why we were born in a particular place, and what social, cultural, and environmental influences have impacted our lives. The older we get, the more we understand how much our lives have been impacted by the previous generation.

Earlier generations – As we continue to move backward in time, we come to the years prior to the birth of all people who are alive today. Yet, we know much about those years through the written histories of them. Those histories help us understand how deeply our lives have been influenced by events and ideas of the past. Our nation, our culture, our families, our attitudes and world-view, and much more are directly shaped by the history of those prior generations, all the way through recorded history (including biblical history) back to the moment of creation.

Pre-history – There was a time, in real history, prior to which nothing existed except for the triune God. We would know nothing about it unless that God Himself revealed it to us. He has not told us much, but He has told us some things. One is that He is "from everlasting." He has always existed. This eternal God has revealed Himself in the pages of Scripture, entered human history in the person of Jesus Christ, and redeemed us. He is responsible for the creation of the universe, and He is also responsible for making us a "new creation."

2 Corinthians 5:17

Therefore if anyone is in Christ, he is a new creation; the old things passed away; behold, new things have come.

He existed since eternity past, created everything, re-created us, and will re-create the heavens and earth. We enter into His eternity going forward, to everlasting, but only He is from everlasting. Apart from His revelation, we could know none of this.

We can understand who, what, and where we are at this point in history by looking not only to the past but to the Creator who is from everlasting to everlasting. We are His created beings who have been re-created in Christ, and we reside in His created cosmos and will dwell in His new creation eternally.

RESPOND TO IT

1. Do the illustrations from mathematics help explain God's eternality and earth's temporality? Do you have another way of explaining these things?

2. Agree/Disagree: The Bible predicts that the end of the earth and the creation of the new heavens and new earth will happen suddenly. This is modeled on the Bible's descriptions of original creation, thus demonstrating that original creation likewise was a sudden event.

15
THE CREATOR
PRESENCE

*Creation matters because it shows that God
has not left us alone.*

Isaiah 43:1
*But now, thus says the LORD, your Creator, O Jacob,
And He who formed you, O Israel,
"Do not fear, for I have redeemed you;
I have called you by name; you are Mine!*

Isaiah 43:7
*Everyone who is called by My name,
And whom I have created for My glory,
Whom I have formed, even whom I have made."*

Isaiah 43:15
*"I am the LORD, your Holy One,
The Creator of Israel, your King."*

Isaiah 43:21
*"The people whom I formed for Myself,
Will declare My praise.*

Isaiah 44:24
*Thus says the LORD, your Redeemer, and the one who formed you
from the womb,*

"I, the LORD, am the maker of all things,
Stretching out the heavens by Myself
And spreading out the earth all alone.

The god of the Deists is a divine creator, with limitations; he has been likened to a divine watchmaker. He made everything, wound it up, set it into motion, and then stepped back, allowing it to wind down according to the laws and principles he built into it. That god remains aloof to this day.

The God of the Bible is the divine Creator, and without limitations. He made everything and put it into motion, but He remains intimately involved with His creation. In Isaiah 43:1 we see this, as we do on almost every page of Scripture. As the involved Creator, His purposes are to reveal Himself and redeem people.

Isaiah did not engage in vague or philosophical God-talk. Rather, he used concrete terms to tell his readers concrete truths about their God who was anything but aloof. According to Isaiah, the doctrine of creation is tightly connected to God's involvement in His creation. Isaiah demonstrated this in at least five ways:

First, the Lord is the Creator of the people of Israel. He says this repeatedly in chapters 43 and 44. In the verses quoted above Isaiah connects the creative activity of the Lord with His present involvement in His people's lives.

Israel existed because God created them as a special people. Lest we think that this implies that God was a territorial god who had just one special clan or nation that He lorded over, Isaiah spelled out the foundational truth behind these statements in 44:24. Specifically, God had done a special creation, namely forming Israel, which He modeled after His universal creation. He did both creations without help or cooperation, the latter for the purpose of revealing Himself and His salvation to all mankind. Just a couple chapters earlier Isaiah declared that the Lord, the Creator of the heavens and the earth, would raise up from Israel One who would bring redemption to all nations:

Isaiah 42:5-7

5 Thus says God the LORD,

Who created the heavens and stretched them out,

Who spread out the earth and its offspring, Who gives breath to the people on it

And spirit to those who walk in it, 6

"I am the LORD, I have called You in righteousness,

I will also hold You by the hand and watch over You,

And I will appoint You as a covenant to the people,

As a light to the nations,

7 To open blind eyes, To bring out prisoners from the dungeon

And those who dwell in darkness from the prison."

Second, the Creator God is involved in the here and now. He may be outside time, but He is clearly involved in real time. Isaiah said in 43:1, "now," not "always." That was intentional. The word "always" would have connoted an eternal principle. While it is an eternal principle that we should not fear for the Lord has redeemed us, Isaiah intended something slightly different. Lest we think that God is outside time and space and therefore unaffected by the events in our lives, the little word "now" corrects that misunderstanding. He acts in real time, in His creation, and for the good of His chosen ones.

Third, God communicates with humans in human language – "thus says the Lord, your Creator." He used words to speak the universe into existence, and He continues to speak to the residents of His universe. He revealed Himself to His creation using the same method He used to create it – words. Because of that, we know His words have power and authority. His words are understandable because they are in human language. He did not require that we try to accommodate our inadequate human language to mystical experiences with Him; rather, He accommodated Himself to us by speaking to us in known human languages. This also reflects our being made in His image – He communicates and we hear; we communicate and He hears.

Fourth, He is the "LORD," translated from "*YHWH*" in the original Hebrew, which means "the ever-existent one," or more simply "the eternal I am." He just is. He is uncreated; He has no birthday; He always was and always will be. He is God; He is Creator; He is eternal. No other so-called god even comes close to Him. Furthermore, we are not God; we are created; we are finite. If He were not *YHWH*, He would be a lesser god.

Fifth, this eternal Creator is intensely personal and intimate with His people. People have a unique place in His creation, and He has called out certain ones to be His own and He has named them (Isaiah 43:1). He has redeemed them, He knows their fears, and He assures them that He is working for their benefit. He is not merely nearby or partially involved. As our Creator, He is intimate with us and totally involved.

RESPOND TO IT

1. To what extent are you a practicing diest?
2. What evidence has occurred in your own life that shows you God has not left you alone?

16
THE CREATOR
PURPOSE

*Creation matters because it shows us
that everything God does is for His glory.*

Isaiah 43:7
*Everyone who is called by My name,
And whom I have created for My glory,
Whom I have formed, even whom I have made."*

Isaiah 43:10-13, 21
*10 "You are My witnesses," declares the LORD,
"And My servant whom I have chosen,
So that you may know and believe Me
And understand that I am He.
Before Me there was no God formed,
And there will be none after Me.
11 "I, even I, am the LORD,
And there is no savior besides Me.
12 "It is I who have declared and saved and proclaimed,
And there was no strange god among you;
So you are My witnesses," declares the LORD,
"And I am God.
13"Even from eternity I am He,
And there is none who can deliver out of My hand;*

I act and who can reverse it?"

... 21"The people whom I formed for Myself Will declare My praise."

Isaiah 42:5, 8

5Thus says God the LORD,
Who created the heavens and stretched them out,
Who spread out the earth and its offspring,
Who gives breath to the people on it
And spirit to those who walk in it."...
8"I am the LORD, that is My name;
I will not give My glory to another,
Nor My praise to graven images.

Isaiah 44:24

Thus says the LORD, your Redeemer, and the one who formed you from the womb,
"I, the LORD, am the maker of all things,
Stretching out the heavens by Myself
And spreading out the earth all alone."

All of creation and everything God has done, is doing, and ever will do have a single purpose – show His glory.

The word "glory" means much more than super-bright or fabulous. We use the word of things besides God – sunsets, coronations, certain landscapes, etc. But God possesses glory unlike and superior to any created thing. In the Bible, the root word means literally "heavy." From that, the word came to denote great value and importance. Therefore, God alone is supremely valuable and important, and the primary reason is that He made everything.

God created Israel. He did so based on His original creation of all things and all people. The verses quoted above are addressed to Israel and frame this larger message.

Since Isaiah's message is couched in creation language rather than in references to Israel's specific history, we can rightfully assume that God is addressing all of humanity through the nation of Israel. What He says to Israel as their Creator, He says to everyone as our Creator. So, the question is, what does He want us to know? To answer that question, consider a few historical examples.

Michelangelo, Johann Sebastian Bach, Thomas Edison, and Leo Tolstoy – What do they all have in common? This: They are all admired for their creative genius and accomplishments. In a real way, their creations bring a certain level of glory to their creators. Isaiah 43:7 says that this is precisely why God created Israel and everything else – to bring glory to Him.

This is crucial; it affects the way we see ourselves and everything. We think He did it for our sake; He didn't; He did it for His own sake. God said repeatedly in Scripture, "I acted for the sake of My name."

God made us, formed us, created us, and called us. Why? For His glory. Period. This does not mean that He never does anything for our benefit. In fact, He has gone to great lengths through Jesus Christ to lavish the unfathomable riches of redemption and forgiveness on us, but we need to remember that even those things He has done primarily for His glory. Everything He has ever done, everything that He is currently doing, and everything that He will ever do is for the purpose of His glory. Until we believe that this is really true, we will never understand God's ways.

Psalm 19:1 says that "the heavens are telling the glory of God." They are not telling the glory of the cosmos, nor are they telling the magnificence of human beings. Neither are they telling the glory of the gods. All creation points to the one true Creator God.

If there were other gods, if there were other creators, or if any divine being assisted in creation, then the Lord would be an egomaniacal deity, because He would be claiming that He did something by Himself when, in fact, He was only partly responsible. This was not a small-scale feat; it was the creation of the entire universe and everything in it. That is why He would be egomaniacal, and rather frightening. But, since there is no other god, and since He alone made everything, it makes sense that He, and He alone, should receive glory. That is the point of Isaiah 43:10-13.

We admire the works of Michelangelo, Bach, Edison, and Tolstoy, but we don't worship them as gods. Why? Because they were finite; they each had a beginning and an end. On the other hand, the Lord is infinite and eternal; but His creation is finite and temporal. He always existed and has always been glorious. He is the original and only God and we live in an original universe created by Him and for Him.

Therefore, just as Israel was created to give Him glory, so are we all created to give Him glory. That is why we exist. That is why creation matters.

RESPOND TO IT

1. Agree/Disagree: Everything God has ever done, is doing, and ever will do is exclusively for His glory.

2. "Glory" is a nice religious word that we associate with God, but what does it actually mean? How would you explain it to a 7-year-old child?

3. Tell about how you have seen the glory of God in creation.

17

THE CREATOR

DIMENSIONS

Creation matters because it is our window to the universe's dimensions.

Ecclesiastes 3:11

He has made everything appropriate in its time. He has also set eternity in their heart, yet so that man will not find out the work which God has done from the beginning even to the end.

Revelation 10:5-6

5 Then the angel whom I saw standing on the sea and on the land lifted up his right hand to heaven, 6 and swore by Him who lives forever and ever, WHO CREATED HEAVEN AND THE THINGS IN IT, AND THE EARTH AND THE THINGS IN IT, AND THE SEA AND THE THINGS IN IT, that there will be delay no longer,

When children are taught that God made everything, they sometimes ask, "But who made God?" the answer is both simple and incomprehensible – No one made God. God always was, is, and always will be. He is eternally existent. That is how He disclosed Himself to Moses in the burning bush: "Tell them I am sent you." There was never a time when God did not exist. And there was never a time when the universe existed apart from Him.

The verses above talk about several things that were created by the eternal God and which exist now but which did not exist prior to some point in the past. The non-Christian looks for naturalistic explanations, but cannot possibly arrive at conclusive answers to all of them. The Bible shines light on things that are not visible to the naturalist.

First, there are three dimensions to space – height, length, and width. These dimensions are obvious to all people. They are not mentioned specifically in Revelation 10:5-6, but they are implicit in the reference to the heavens, earth, and sea. We live in a three-dimensional universe. A dimension is something that can be measured. We can observe, study, and measure these things. The point is that the doctrine of creation is consistent with the observable dimensions which are the same everywhere and at all times, because God Himself built that stability into His creation.

Second, there is also another created dimension, time. Here again, anyone can observe, study, and contemplate time. But there are mysteries associated with time that are beyond mere human understanding. Human reason cannot answer certain questions such as: Was there time before time? Will there be an end of time? Can we step outside time? Does time proceed differently in different parts of the universe? Can time be compressed or expanded? Is time-travel a real possibility or just the stuff of science fiction? The Bible does not address all these questions, but it is very clear about one of them. Before time, there was only the timeless God. But we are created beings in a created universe that is bound by time, so when we look to the eternal God, we do so through the window of time. The Bible does not leave us on our own to speculate about the timeless Creator, but rather uses time-based language to describe His eternality – "forever and ever." Such language at least gives us a glimpse into the eternality of God. We are constrained by the three dimensions of space, but God is not. Likewise, we are constrained by the dimension of time, but God is not.

Nothing we observe exists outside the dimension of time. Light itself is measured in terms of time and space – miles-per-second. Interstellar distances are measured in light-years, the distance light travels in one year. Light cannot be captured motionless in a box. If there is no time, there is no light. All life is measured by time, as everything and everybody has a past, present, and future. All motion depends on time, such as miles-per-hour.

We reside in a four-dimensional universe. That is no great flash of inspirational insight. The unbeliever sees those dimensions and perhaps wonders if there are more, or if those four are unchanging. The believer sees those same dimensions and knows that there is more, much more, outside them, namely the triune God and the entire spiritual realm. We rely on the stability of the dimensions because God made them stable, because He Himself is stable, the theological word for that is "immutable." But, if we live in a universe that is bounded by these observable dimensions and that is therefore finite and measurable, where did the ideas of eternity and infinity come from? That leads to the next point.

Third, the concepts of infinity and eternity did not enter the human race when some brilliant ancient mathematician sat down one day and realized that there are no largest and smallest numbers. Since the earliest days of our existence on earth, we have known that there are such things as eternity and infinity. And, we all have a sneaking suspicion that there is something or Someone outside ourselves that is infinite and eternal. Most of us also suspect that possibly, just possibly, we may exist into eternity. It is the common experience of all people to yearn for that eternal something. It doesn't take a mathematician to put two and two together, looking first at the created universe which speaks to the glory of an eternal Creator, and then looking at our common yearning for something eternal, to reach the conclusion that our internal compass that points to eternity was placed there by that Creator. That truth is what Ecclesiastes. 3:11 affirms.

Fourth, Revelation 3:5-6 is clear that everything – astronomical, geological, oceanographical, biological, and chronological – has been created by God. Everything that we investigate and study – all science, all math, and every other course of study – is an exploration of what God has designed and made. Even studies of diseases and natural disasters are studies of the created ideals which had been corrupted by the fall. The Christian finds great comfort and motivation in that. We are not studying cosmic accidents and inexplicable appearances of life. Because everything has been made by a wise, rational God, we can use our wisdom and reason to explore, study, and interpret our world and universe. Our starting point is the infinite Creator God who opens the window to infinite possibilities. Therefore, the Christian is humble about how thorough and accurate our knowledge is, but is also confident that we are able to gain true knowledge about ourselves and the heavens and the earth. The non-Christian, on the other hand, has only finite self as his or her starting point, and therefore is limited by the finiteness of his or her own mind. For them, truth and reality, if they actually exist, are always wrapped in a cloak of subjectivity.

RESPOND TO IT

1. Time is created; eternity is not. We exist in time; God exists in eternity. We measure all things in terms of width, length, depth, and time. Name some things that we can only understand in terms of time, such as speed, growth, and relationships.

2. How can understanding time in this way provide comfort, encouragement and strength?

3. Discuss the differences between how a Christian approaches science and how a non-Christian does.

18

THE CREATOR
POWER

Creation matters because it is the primary
revelation of God's power.

Jeremiah 10:12
It is He who made the earth by His power,
Who established the world by His wisdom;
And by His understanding He has stretched out the heavens.

Jeremiah 27:5
"I have made the earth, the men and the beasts which are on the face
of the earth by My great power and by My outstretched arm, and I
will give it to the one who is pleasing in My sight.

Jeremiah 32:17
'Ah LORD GOD! Behold, You have made the heavens and the earth
by Your great power and by Your outstretched arm! Nothing is too
difficult for You,

Creation mattered to Jeremiah. It dominated his thoughts about God. It was not merely one doctrine among many. It was foundational to his understanding of the ways of God. It enabled him to understand that the impending invasions and exile of the Jewish people would be exclusively attributable to the will of the Creator. The Lord had made all people and all things, so no nation and no events were out of His control. In fact, they were all under His control. If God could make a universe and all the living creatures, including humans, He could use His power to do whatever pleased Him.

Fast-forward to the present day. Many Christians do not think much about creation apart from times when they are studying, discussing, or debating the issue of creation vs. evolution. The doctrine of creation often has only a passing influence on our thoughts about God. Unfortunately, we could take creation out of the picture, and our thinking about God would not change much. But for Jeremiah, it was the one thread in the tapestry of his prophecy that would have unraveled the whole thing if it were pulled out. For him it was the key for understanding the power of God and how He was working. It still is the key.

Today we believe that God is powerful, and He is. But we are a little muddled about where to see it. We act almost like He is partially powerful or marginally powerful. We would never be so heretical as to say that He is not powerful, but we are just not sure that we are seeing much evidence of His power.

We verbally affirm that He can do powerful things, but realistically we often think He uses His power only occasionally or in little ways. If a few people feel exceptionally close to the Lord in a worship service, they claim that "God showed up in a powerful way." Others pray in clichés, "Lord, be with so-and-so in a powerful way," having no idea what they are actually praying for. We get goosebumps when we hear the "Hallelujah Chorus," For the Lord God omnipotent reigneth," but in the routine of our lives we don't really expect to see much of that. We believe in His power, we want to see His power, but we are not sure where to look. Other things are powerful – armies, weapons, cultural forces, economies, certain politicians, volcanos, hurricanes – but where is the power of God? We witness little things here and there, but nothing that would motivate us to compose something like the "Hallelujah Chorus." We wish that God would do something noticeable, but meanwhile we plod along each day oblivious to His power.

The problem is not that God has retreated from His creation or has become minimally powerful, but that we are partially blind. We are fish swimming around in a lake wondering how to get wet. We are immersed in the power of God and do not even realize it. His power is never partial; it is always absolute and total. A major reason why we are mostly blind to His power is that we have lost sight of creation. This often appears to be an out-of-control world, but when it appears that way to us, the problem is that we are seeing too little, not too much. Jeremiah had 20/20 vision on creation, and consequently he was overwhelmed by the power of God. He understood that as the Creator God was orchestrating everything. Everything that exists is there by God's power. Everything that happens is also by His power.

The take-away is this: We need to do what Jeremiah did – focus on the Creator God. When he did that, Jeremiah found comfort, understanding, and purpose for the events in his life. He had a firm confidence that God could and would use His power to intervene in current events, according to His will and in His timing. He was crystal clear about God's power to do what He wills to do now because of what He has done in the past:

- He created Jeremiah himself -- *"Before I formed you in the womb I knew you,"* (Jer. 1:5)

- He created all mankind – *"For the Maker of all is He,"* (Jer. 10:16)

- He created the earth and its human and animal inhabitants -- *"I have made the earth, the men and the beasts which are on the face of the earth by My great power and by My outstretched arm,"* (Jer. 27:5)

- He created the entirety of everything in the heavens, as well as the earth – *"Ah LORD GOD! Behold, You have made the heavens and the earth by Your great power and by Your outstretched arm! Nothing is too difficult for You,"* (Jer. 32:17)

If we do not have a clear understanding of creation, we will doubt the power of God. If we have a clear understanding of creation, we will see the power of God everywhere, at all times, and in all things.

RESPOND TO IT

1. Agree/Disagree: Most Christians believe in the absolute power of God, but in practice we act like we doubt it.

2. Where should we look to see the power of God?

3. Discuss the implications of these statements from the study: "[Jeremiah] understood that as the Creator of everything, God was orchestrating everything. Everything that exists is there by God's power. Everything that happens is also by His power."

4. Agree/Disagree: If we do not have a clear understanding of creation, we will doubt the power of God.

19
THE CREATOR
RAMIFICATIONS

Creation matters because it determines
who our God will be.

Romans 1:25

For they exchanged the truth of God for a lie, and worshiped and
served the creature rather than the Creator, who is blessed forever.
Amen.

Paul used the doctrine of creation as the basis for his teaching in
which we looked at in study 7, "Implication: Reason and Truth." In
that passage he was showing what happens to people who ignore or
reject the fact that the heavens, earth and everything in them were
created by God. When humans turn away from the Creator, they
invariably turn to the creation. This leads to idolatry, moral decay,
and anarchy.

A central point of the passage is this — If we do not acknowledge
and honor god as the Creator, we can do whatever we want with our
bodies and marry whomever we want. In fact, we can do whatever
we want.

All the sins in Romans 1:20-32 are what happens when: (1) people
reject God as Creator, (2) make themselves the god of their own
lives, and (3) see the physical world as all that there is. Therefore,
rejection of the Creator is not simply a philosophical or religious
topic. It is the root cause of the collapse of individuals and societies,
sometimes quickly, sometimes over generations.

This is a matter of enormous importance for Christians living in

America. We need to understand that fornication, homosexuality, idolatry, and all the other vices listed in Romans 1:28-32 are not just violations of moral standards. They are violations of the nature of creation itself and its Creator. For that reason, when the passage brings up homosexuality in verses 26-27, it is not just as a moral issue; in fact, that is secondary. Primarily it is a violation of God's creation-design for human beings. Christians cannot support homosexual practices and same-sex marriage, partly for moral reasons, but mostly for creation reasons.

Homosexual behavior is wrong because it rejects the design and the Designer of human beings. To repeat: this is a creation issue more than a moral issue. At creation, God made human beings, and only human beings, in His image. He made them male and female, suitable for each other. He did not give Adam an animal companion, nor did He give him a husband. He gave him a wife. He gave Eve a husband, not a wife. He gave them each other in a male-female, husband-wife relationship to embody His image. This is why the Bible forbids homosexuality – it is contrary to our creation as human beings. It is contrary to the image of God.

Likewise, all the other sins in Romans 1:20-32 are what happen when people reject the Creator and the doctrine of creation. It is why Christians must not neglect this doctrine, lest we become vulnerable to these sins. Romans 1:20-32 shows the disarray that eventually happens in the lives of those who ignore or reject creation. In the thinking of unbelievers, those sins go from tolerable, to acceptable, to approved, to celebrated. Right-and-wrong, good-and-bad, moral-and-immoral are turned inside-out. The evidence is multi-faceted – envy, murder, strife, malice, hatred of God, insolence, slander, arrogance, mercilessness, and self-absorption, *"and they give hearty approval to those who practice them,"* Romans 1:32. At that point, the people who do not embrace these behaviors are likely to be maligned or even persecuted.

So far we have been looking at the negative results of rejecting the Creator and the fact of creation. Romans 1:25 also tells us several positive things about believing in the Creator.

First, there is the "truth of God." Truth is not something we invent or subjectively choose, but it is a combination of observations, interpretations, understanding, and conclusions that correspond to reality. Truth is built into creation which in turn reveals certain true things about the Creator. These are not relative, subjective, personal truths, but concrete ones. There is objective reality that tells us objectively true things about creation and, by implication, about the Creator .

Second, He rather than His creation is to be worshiped. Everyone who sees the majesty and intricacy of the created order should be driven to their knees in awe and worship of the Creator. The path to clear thinking is to see creation as God's handiwork and to worship Him.

Third, the Creator is "blessed." He is both the source and the object of blessing. From Him flows all the goodness, i.e. blessings, of creation because that is how He created everything originally – "good," as repeated several times in Gen. 1. In that sense He blesses creation which in turn ought to bless Him. We are not to attempt to make God feel blessed, but to admire and praise His goodness. To bless God is to speak rightly and truly about Him and His goodness, leading others to likewise praise Him.

Fourth, God is "forever," eternal. He created time; He existed before time; He is outside of time; He is also involved in time; He will exist when time is no more. If He were not forever, He would merely be like us, only more so, but He would be bound by the same limitations, regressions, and constraints of time that bind us – beginnings, aging, deteriorating, and ending. But because He is forever, He does not grow, age, learn, develop, change, or come to an end.

Fifth, He is apart from His creation. He is not coterminous with creation. We are creatures, while He is Creator. We are not God or an extension of Him, but we are made by God in His image, so He is separate from us, but not detached from us. We are not one with God, and yet God is with us. He is not us, but He made us. In creation He has bridged time and eternity. His forever-ness and our created-ness in His image foreshadow our hope for eternal life.

In conclusion, Romans 1:20-32 tells us both how things ought to be if we believe in the Creator, and how they are if we reject the Creator. We either bow before Him as God, or we designate ourselves to be god and/or worship creation. One path leads to eternal life, the other to depravity and death.

RESPOND TO IT

1. Agree/Disagree: "If God is not the Creator, we can do whatever we want with our bodies and marry whomever we want. In fact, we can do whatever we want."

2. Discuss: "Christians cannot support homosexual practices and same-sex marriage, partly for moral reasons, but mostly for creation reasons."

3. How can we "bless" God?

20
THE CREATOR
SUFFERING

*Creation matters because it
sustains us through suffering.*

1 Peter 4:19

*Therefore, those also who suffer according to the will of God shall
entrust their souls to a faithful Creator in doing what is right.*

This is one of those verses about our Creator that can slip right
past us. It is in the context of telling us how to respond rightly
to suffering. Peter draws our attention to the fact that suffering is
according to God's will, so we need to entrust our souls to Him and
live righteously. It is easy to miss two essential words in the verse:
"faithful Creator."

For Peter, the idea of God as Creator was near the front of his
mind as he comforted and instructed his readers about suffering.
If we were writing about that, we would probably refer to God as
our rock, our shepherd, our fortress, our strength, our sovereign
Lord, or something along those lines. Peter, instead, refers to the
Lord as "a faithful Creator," rather than as "our faithful Creator."
In using that phrase, he was not saying that God is one of several
gods or one of several creators. Rather, he was saying that "faithful
Creator" defines who God is. Peter's message was this – In the
midst of acute or prolonged troubles and suffering, we need to
remember, above all else, that God is a faithful Creator, He is the
guardian of His creation, and therefore we are constantly under
His care. The suffering we experience is not random; it is not a
surprise to God. Rather in some mysterious way our Creator is

carrying out His will, even in our suffering.

Why should the thought of God as Creator sustain us through suffering? There are several reasons:

First, God is in control. Our suffering is according to His will, not according to hostile forces outside His jurisdiction. He is orchestrating the circumstances of our lives, so even when things look bleak we can be assured that the infinitely wise and powerful Creator God is behind, above, and in it all. We wish His will did not include suffering, and this is not an easy topic to understand, but since the Bible says it is so, we need to look at the bigger picture. From small to large and from brief to prolonged, our suffering is in the hands of the powerful Creator. His love and care are forever "faithful." No matter how bad things get, His faithful care never ceases.

Second, there is nothing that He did not create. Creation was not partially done by God and partially by some other deity or cosmic force. Therefore, no matter how distressing things are, apart from sin there is nothing that is alien to the Lord. Even though evil, suffering, and death entered creation when Adam and Eve sinned, God was not caught off-guard without a plan. He remains the sovereign Lord, which means that everything, our suffering included, was within His purview from the time of creation. In ways that we cannot completely understand, He even uses the wicked things that people do to accomplish His purposes. We see that in the story of Joseph when he confronted his brothers after they sold him into slavery: *"As for you, you meant evil against me, but God meant it for good in order to bring about this present result, to preserve many people alive,"* Genesis 50:20.

Third, the Creator sets the rules. The founder of a business determines how the business should be conducted by the employees. An inventor has the sole right to tell people how the invention should be used. The Creator of the world has explained how to do the "right" things in the "right" way, and He expects us to follow those instructions. However, He is not sitting in heaven wringing His hands in frustration when His instructions are not followed or when we suffer. He is working out His will in all circumstances.

Fourth, God is a faithful Creator. Peter could have just called God "the Creator," and that would have been sufficient. But he added the word "faithful." What is Peter saying to us? One of the things he wants us to keep in mind is that we should not be fooled and distressed by appearances. Even when things seem bad, we can rely on the reality that our Creator God continues to be faithful. He faithfully made the world and everything in it; He faithfully made us a new creation; He faithfully is keeping us for the day of Christ's return; and He is faithfully governing all that goes on in our lives and in the world.

We may make passing references to God as Creator, but we rarely reflect on the significance of that. This truth becomes very important to us when we suffer and struggle to find our way. If we lose sight of our starting point, and if we are not sure where we are going, we will wander aimlessly, hoping that maybe the invisible, marginally involved God will step in and do something. In reality, that is how many of us think. In 1 Peter, Peter is trying to help us regain our perspective. He reminds us where we started, where we are going, and how we should live in the meantime. Over all, God is the Creator, and He is faithful, not just in general, but toward us...always.

RESPOND TO IT

1. Creation seems like such an academic subject. In realistic terms, how can it be a comfort to all of us when we go through difficult times? Can you relate how this truth sustained you through a difficult time?

2. How can suffering be "according to the will of God?" How can knowing that be a comfort?

21
THE CREATOR
Helper

*Creation matters because it is the
reason that God is our help.*

Psalm 121:2
*My help comes from the LORD,
Who made heaven and earth.*

Psalm 124:8
*Our help is in the name of the LORD,
Who made heaven and earth.*

Psalm 138:8
*The LORD will accomplish what concerns me;
Your lovingkindness, O LORD, is everlasting;
Do not forsake the works of Your hands.*

No one doubts that God is our "help." We happily affirm it when things are going well, and we generally agree with it when we encounter short-term difficult patches. But when things get really rough for prolonged periods of time, that's when we struggle emotionally and wonder if He is really up to the job. We probably would never verbalize it like that, but in our hearts we are thinking it. The thing we need to think about is why we believe that He is our help. For many of us, we believe it because the Bible says so, and that is a good reason. But when distress and grief hit us, His help described in the Bible starts to feel distant and too-little-too-late. That happens when we view His help as just one more item on a list of the things that God does. We need to look deeper, specifically at what the verses above tell us about God's help.

He helps us because of who He is, not because of who we are or because it is a task on His divine "To-Do" list. Likewise, God does not help His people as a sort of divine babysitter or bodyguard. He is much more than that. If that is all He is, He would be helping someone else's creation, but that is not the case. This is His world and we are His people, and He is helping His own creation. No other so-called god and no other created being has such creative power and such knowledge. Therefore, God can be and is our help because, and only because, He made heaven and earth and everything in them. As the Creator, He cares about His creation and especially about us, people who are made in His image and redeemed by Him.

He can and does intervene in His creation all the time, not just sometimes, even if we do not detect it with our senses. This is why we should not merely hope and pray that God will help us from time to time. Rather, because He is the Creator, we rely on His help every moment.

This is why the well-intentioned expression "It was a God-thing" is misleading. It implies that God gets involved occasionally but not constantly. Everything is a God-thing. He does not just "show up" now and then. We do not need to try to do "God-sightings" as if His help was unusual or barely detectable. He is the ever-present Creator whose help is total and ongoing. Without His "help" none of us would be able to draw our next breath or think our next thought.

He constantly accomplishes what concerns us. We may or may not be aware of His help, and in fact, it is usually unnoticed. It is in both the ordinary and the extraordinary events of our lives. It is there in our interactions with others, in the choices we make throughout each day, and in the strength we need minute-by-minute. He is not a once-in-a-while helper. He always sustains us and always has us in His loving care. He does that because He made us. When we think about His help, we should always think about why He is our help, namely that He is our Creator. As such He is powerful, eternal, loving, wise, and involved.

RESPOND TO IT

1. When we talk about helping someone, we think in terms of "lending a hand" to support the person. How is this like and unlike the Lord being our "help?"

2. Discuss why our thinking about the Lord can be misled by expressions like "It was a God-Thing" and "Then God showed up."

3. Agree/Disagree: "But when things get really rough for prolonged periods of time, that's when we struggle emotionally and wonder if He is really up to the job."

4. "We do not need to try to do 'God-sightings' as if His help was unusual or barely detectable. He is the ever-present Creator whose help is thorough and ongoing." If this is true, where should we be looking to see God's help?

22

THE CREATOR

MOCKERS

*Creation matters because it gives insight
into the thinking of mockers.*

2 Peter 3:3-10

3 Know this first of all, that in the last days mockers will come with their mocking, following after their own lusts, 4 and saying, "Where is the promise of His coming? For ever since the fathers fell asleep, all continues just as it was from the beginning of creation." 5 For when they maintain this, it escapes their notice that by the word of God the heavens existed long ago and the earth was formed out of water and by water, 6 through which the world at that time was destroyed, being flooded with water. 7 But by His word the present heavens and earth are being reserved for fire, kept for the day of judgment and destruction of ungodly men.

8 But do not let this one fact escape your notice, beloved, that with the Lord one day is like a thousand years, and a thousand years like one day. 9 The Lord is not slow about His promise, as some count slowness, but is patient toward you, not wishing for any to perish but for all to come to repentance.

10 But the day of the Lord will come like a thief, in which the heavens will pass away with a roar and the elements will be destroyed with intense heat, and the earth and its works will be burned up.

Peter's warnings in these verses are based on the three most important events in the history of the world — Creation, Jesus Christ, and the end of the world. The first and third of these are the bookends of time; the second of them is the focal point of earth history between those bookends. Peter tells us that in the closing days of earth's history, there will be mockers of a special sort. These will be secular humanists, people who think of themselves as realists or pragmatists or anti-supernaturalists, who know just enough about the Bible and Jesus Christ to jeer at those who are true believers. These mockers will know that Christians believe, or ought to believe, in the future second coming of Christ, but because so much time will have passed by then, they will ridicule Christians, saying things like, "Get real! He's not returning!" (v. 4). They also will know that Christians believe, or ought to believe, in creation. They will throw that in our faces, jeeringly pointing out that we live in a world governed by the laws of nature where everything always goes along as it always has (v. 4), implying that everything that happens is explainable by natural causes and that supernatural intervention never occurred and never will.

These mockers rightly understand that Christians accept by faith what happened and what will happen at the bookends of time. Neither bookend is knowable by scientific observation or by reason, but only by revelation from God. But the mockers reject God, so they also reject revelation and the ideas of creation and Christ's return.

As Peter described these future mockers — are we already seeing them? — he told us two important things about them. First, they are motivated by their own lusts (v. 3) rather than by genuine doubts and intellectual conclusions. Their mockery of Christians' belief in creation and the Lord's return is a façade covering their true motives and lusts. They know that faith in Christ, belief in creation, and the expectation of Jesus' second coming are inconsistent with their cravings, opinions, and lifestyles, so they deride Christian beliefs as ridiculous.

The second thing Peter notes about the mockers is that they refuse to acknowledge what every human is aware of at some level – namely that the heavens and earth are the work of a supernatural Being. They should at least have an inkling about this. Peter is echoing Paul's teaching in Romans 1:18-25. Both apostles assert that every human being has a rudimentary knowledge that there is a God who is the Creator of the heavens, earth, and seas.

We need to remember that while people do have genuine questions about creation and faith in Christ, much of the modern disdain for our beliefs stems from something besides intellectual or scientific questions. Often it stems from the motives and lifestyles of the critics. Intellectual arguments often disguise something deeper, namely lusts for things that are contrary to biblical teaching. Unbelief may actually be a moral issue rather than an intellectual one.

Twice in these verses Peter refers to the "word of God." In verse 5 he reaffirms the basic fact that all of creation came into existence through God's word. Everyone should notice that, although the mockers are blind to it. Then, in verse 7 he writes that the current heavens and earth are preserved by His word. God's method of preserving is exactly His same method of creating – He speaks, and it is so. The world was created by His word — the first bookend. One day the world will end by His word — the final bookend. We continue to exist between the bookends in precisely the same way — by His word. We must never think that God set things in motion and then stepped back until He shows up again to finish things. We also must never think that His method for sustaining and controlling His creation is any different from the method by which He created and will terminate everything.

RESPOND TO IT

1. When we talk to a non-Christian, are there any ways by which we can discern whether their unbelief is a matter of intellectual doubt, ignorance, or moral willfulness?

2. Why does 2 Peter 3:7 say that the present heavens and earth are preserved by His "word" rather than by His power?

3. Are we already seeing the mockers predicted by Peter? If so, describe them. How can we talk to them?

23
THE CREATOR
REST

*Creation matters because it is the
only reason for the Sabbath.*

Hebrews 4:4

*For He has said somewhere concerning the seventh day: "AND GOD
RESTED ON THE SEVENTH DAY FROM ALL HIS WORKS."*

The Sabbath is a big deal throughout Scripture. It is so important that God encoded it in the Ten Commandments: *Remember the Sabbath day to keep it holy,* Exodus 20:8. This is where creation and the Law intersect. In Hebrews 4, the Sabbath is infused with new significance, referring to the rest that believers enter into by faith in the gospel. Verses 9-10 say: *9 So there remains a Sabbath rest for the people of God. 10 For the one who has entered His rest has himself also rested from his works, as God did from His.* So, the weekly observance of the Sabbath in the Old Testament foreshadowed the eternal Sabbath that believers enter into, beginning the moment they trust Christ.

The commandment to "remember the Sabbath day to keep it holy" was never rescinded. Christians should continue to observe a Sabbath day in recognition of this eternal reality. Most modern Christians seem to treat the Sabbath as the one commandment out of the Ten that no longer applies. While each of us violates all Ten in one way or another, we especially have little or no regard for keeping the Sabbath. Realistically, most modern Christians believe in the Nine Commandments.

Some minimize the Sabbath for cultural or pragmatic reasons. We have no agreed-upon day of the week that we all call the Sabbath, although most Christians probably identify Sunday as that day. But even acknowledging that, realistically we are so busy and have so much to do every day that we cannot imagine devoting one whole day entirely to worshiping God, resting, fellowshipping, and eating. It is an unusual Christian who consistently reserves Sundays for just these things.

Others minimize it for theological reasons. Specifically, they assume that our eternal Sabbath has displaced the weekly Sabbath. They find Hebrews 4 to be the justification for their view. However, the text does not say that the weekly Sabbath no longer applies. If anything, as mentioned above, the weekly Sabbath reinforces and illustrates our eternal Sabbath. It does so in three ways.

First, when Christians set apart one day a week as a Sabbath, it is a tangible reminder for us of who God is and what He has done – He created everything, provided salvation, and initiated eternal rest. Additionally, non-Christians may eventually notice that their Christian friends are treating one day a week differently from the others and realize that there is something very real and important that would cause someone to do something so countercultural. In other words, a Christian who practices a Sabbath rest is a road-sign pointing to Jesus Christ.

Second, observing a Sabbath day is a weekly reminder to Christians about creation. The historical precedent for the Sabbath was God's "rest" on the seventh day of the creation week. That precedent is the stated purpose for the commandment in Exodus 20:11 – *For in six days the LORD made the heavens and the earth, the sea and all that is in them, and rested on the seventh day; therefore the LORD blessed the Sabbath day and made it holy.* In the daily grind of our lives, we can easily lose sight of the reality that this world is the creation of God. The Sabbath returns our thinking to the fact that we are created beings residing in a created world. And because we are created in God's image, we logically should follow the pattern that He established for us at creation. Perhaps this is a significant reason why Christians don't give much thought to creation: On the whole we have abandoned the weekly, tangible reminder about creation that God has given us. It's like this: When we observe a Sabbath day, we should ask ourselves, "Why are we doing this?" There are two answers that overshadow all others – One, because God created everything in six days and rested on the seventh and commanded us to do so, and two, God has given us an eternal Sabbath through faith in Jesus Christ.

Third, as the commandment itself states, since God rested on the seventh day following His creation-work in the preceding six days, so we should rest after six days of work. God has wired us to rest one day a week, every week. When God rested at the end of the creation week, He was not exhausted, needing to recoup His energy. Rather, He was ceasing the work in which He was engaged the prior six days. As we learn from this fourth Commandment, He was also establishing a pattern for us. It does not matter how strong we feel or how much we have to do, we should rest one day a week. God had the entirety of creation to attend to, yet He rested. We can infer that His message to us is: "Rest. Don't worry. You will get your stuff done in six days." It's like He is giving us 52 vacation days every year.

The question of what is and what is not permitted on a Sabbath day is a topic for another book, although most of us can use some biblical common sense to figure that out. Also, this is not turning a blind eye to the realities of life in contemporary America. We are all busy, and there are many things that we like to do on Sundays. So, it will take a significant readjustment in our thinking and lifestyles to start setting Sundays (or some other regular day each week) aside for worship, rest, fellowship, and eating. The point here is that we have a choice: we actually can set aside one day a week for these purposes, and take care of everything else on the other six days.

There are still Ten Commandments, not nine, and the fourth one about the Sabbath keeps the doctrine of creation front and center in our minds. Perhaps the major reason why many Christians don't think much about creation is that the Sabbath is not very important to us. And, perhaps the reason that the Sabbath is not very important to us is that we don't think much about creation.

RESPOND TO IT

1. Agree/Disagree: Keeping the Sabbath is just as relevant for Christians today as is keeping the other nine Commandments.

2. Agree/Disagree: Perhaps the major reason why many Christians don't think much about creation is that the Sabbath is not very important to us. And, perhaps the reason that the Sabbath is not very important to us is that we don't think much about creation.

3. How realistic is it for us to keep the Sabbath? How would the average Christian do that?

24
THE CREATOR
Our Maker

Creation matters because God alone,
not nature, made us.

Over and over the Scriptures refer to God as our "Maker." [1] He wants us to be crystal clear about this. This tells us who and what we are. All humans are made by the direct activity of God. We procreate, but we do not make ourselves.

Genesis 1:27
God created man in His own image, in the image of God He created him; male and female He created them.

Psalm 100:3
It is He who has made us, and not we ourselves.

Psalm 139:13
For You formed my inward parts;
You wove me in my mother's womb.

Humans are a special creation made by God, originally and currently.

Knowing that God set up the whole process of procreation when He originally made Adam and Eve, many Christians seem to think that subsequently He is letting nature take its course. But this idea contradicts passages like the ones quoted above. God made Adam out of the dust of the ground, and then He made Eve from Adam's

---

1. A few of these verses are: Job 4:17, 32:22, 35:10, 36:3, 40:19; Psa. 95:6, 119:73, 149:2; Prov. 14:31, 17:5, 22:2; Isa. 17:7, 27:11, 29:16, 44:24, 45:9, 45:11, 51:13, 54:5; Jer. 10:16, 51:19; Hos. 8:14.

rib. Those were unique acts of creation, never to be repeated. But that does not mean that God is uninvolved in the formation of every human since then. He continues to oversee everything about us – our conception, development in the womb, birth, life, and death. He is not just a passive observer. He decides when we will be born, who our parents will be, what we will look like, and what personality we will have. Something grand and mysterious is happening in the development of every human baby – a new human being is being formed in the womb, and God is overseeing the process.

If you are a skilled crafts-person and you make something from scratch, you know what is involved in that. You start with an idea, develop a design and a plan, obtain the raw materials, fashion and assemble the item, and put on the finishing touches. Then you step back and assess your work, and if you like it, you smile, and put it on display or put it into use for its intended purpose. That object reflects your skill, intelligence, and creativity. In short, it brings glory to you. That is what was going on when God created us. We are made in His image and so we reflect His skill, intelligence, and creativity. (Gen. 1:26-27, 2:7), and we should bring glory to Him.

Therefore, throughout the Bible, it's as if God keeps telling us to not forget that we did not just happen but that we were made by Him in His image, and therefore we have dignity and purpose. Whatever we may believe about the age of the earth, the one thing all Christians should believe is that humans are the special creation of God. The life we have is different from all other forms of life on this planet. Our life was breathed into us by God (Gen. 2:7) rather than inherited from a pre-human ancestor.

A Christian is free to believe that humans evolved from lower forms of life. But, in holding that belief, he or she needs to be honest enough to admit that he or she does not believe the Bible on this point. This is more than a matter of interpreting Genesis 1-2, it is a matter of believing what the rest of Scripture tells us about human beings. All the "Maker" verses are Scripture's own commentary on Genesis 1-2. Whether you believe in an old earth or a young earth, the Scriptures compel us to believe that at some specific point in the past, God did something unique – He made human beings special and separate from all other life on earth. And even now, every human being that is born is special and separate from all other life on earth. There are no exceptions. Each of us is a unique design by an infinitely creative Creator.

RESPOND TO IT

1. How might you use this study and the verses quoted to counsel and encourage someone who is struggling with self-image.

2. Agree/Disagree: "A Christian is free to believe that humans evolved from lower forms of life. But, in holding that belief, he or she needs to be honest enough to admit that he or she does not believe the Bible on this point."

3. How would you use the verses above to defend a pro-life position?

25
THE CREATOR
METHODOLOGY

*Creation matters because it shows
the power of God's word.*

Genesis 1:3-26

Then God said, "Let there be...,
...and it was so.

(8 times in these verses, with minor variations in the wording)

Psalm 33:6

By the word of the LORD the heavens were made,
And by the breath of His mouth all their host.

Psalm 33:9

For He spoke, and it was done;
He commanded, and it stood fast.

Psalm 148:4-6

4Praise Him, highest heavens,
And the waters that are above the heavens!

5 Let them praise the name of the LORD, For He commanded and
they were created.
6 He has also established them forever and ever;
He has made a decree which will not pass away.

Hebrews 11:3

By faith we understand that the worlds were prepared by the word of God, so that what is seen was not made out of things which are visible.

Romans 4:17

(as it is written, "A father of many nations have I made you") in the presence of Him whom he believed, even God, who gives life to the dead and calls into being that which does not exist.

Several years ago I heard a brilliant science professor from a prestigious university speak at a church on the topic of creation. This man was a devoted Christian, and he was attempting to show that there is no ultimate conflict between true science and the Bible. Several times during his series of messages he said: "The Bible teaches only that God created, not how He created." As a scientist, he was trying to persuade the congregation to be willing to accept the conclusions of science (especially evolution) even when they seem to contradict Scripture. But his argument neglected the fact that actually the Bible repeatedly says how God created, namely He spoke everything into existence. How did God create? He spoke.

This truth raises several important points.

First, according to Psalm 33:6, God used words to make everything we see above us in the heavens. Words express thoughts and intentions. God had a design in mind, and He verbalized it, and His design came into being. Those words had power; they were not just concepts. The initial physical universe was exactly what God had in mind. It was all His design. God's creation-words were unlike human words in this respect. We cannot speak things into existence. When we imagine, design, plan, and build things, we use words all along the way. In that regard we are expressing something of the image of God. But we can never merely speak and create something out of nothing, because our words do not possess creative power.

Second, this leads us to the doctrine of "creation ex nihilo," namely that God created everything out of nothing. God began with nothing physical, as Romans 4:17 and Hebrews 11:3 assert. This is the basic difference between the Bible's teaching and the "Big Bang" theory. In the beginning there was nothing, absolutely nothing, except the triune God. There was no tiny amount of physical matter, no time, no physical dimensions, no physical life, no empty space, and no physical energy. There was only God. He spoke, and the universe came into existence.

Third, Hebrews 11:3 gives us an additional insight into the how of creation. Specifically, it is a matter of faith rather than of demonstrable scientific proof. We can see evidences that God created everything, but we can never have irrefutable physical proof of it. This is where secular scientists are at a disadvantage. They can only speculate about the origins of the universe, but they can never really know what happened. They are boxed in by the limits of their finite human reasoning, intelligence, and ability to observe. Christians have those same limitations, but with one notable exception: We believe that there is a God and that He has spoken to us in the pages of Scripture. In those pages He revealed to us that He spoke, and the entire known universe came into being. We understand and accept that by faith, not by reason, although it is not contrary to reason. In fact, it is completely reasonable.

Fourth, the Genesis 1 narrative says repeatedly, "God said, 'Let there be...and it was so.'" This is the Bible's explanation for the origin of everything, both animate and inanimate. We know from Scripture that God's method for creating was to speak. He began, controlled, and ordered the entire creation process with words.

Every rock, every star, every tree, every animal, every sea creature, every ocean, every cloud, every atomic particle, every human being is a verbal expression of the mind of God.

RESPOND TO IT

1. Do you agree with the assertion of the college science professor: "The Bible teaches only that God created, not how He created."

2. Today we have "God's word" on the pages of Scripture. How does that relate to God's word as His method of creation?

3. How does this study affect your view of the power of the words of the Bible?

26
THE CREATOR
CREATION'S COMPANION

Creation matters because it reveals God's wisdom.

Psalm 104:24

O LORD, how many are Your works!
In wisdom You have made them all;
The earth is full of Your possessions.

Psalm 136:5-9

5 To Him who made the heavens with skill [i.e., wisdom],
For His lovingkindness is everlasting;
6 To Him who spread out the earth above the waters,
For His lovingkindness is everlasting;
7 To Him who made the great lights,
For His lovingkindness is everlasting:
8The sun to rule by day,
For His lovingkindness is everlasting,
9 The moon and stars to rule by night,
For His lovingkindness is everlasting.

Proverbs 3:19

The LORD by wisdom founded the earth,
By understanding He established the heavens.

Proverbs 8:22-31

22 *"The LORD possessed me [Wisdom] at the beginning of His way, Before His works of old.*

23 *"From everlasting I was established,*

From the beginning, from the earliest times of the earth.

24 *"When there were no depths I was brought forth,*

When there were no springs abounding with water.

25 *"Before the mountains were settled, Before the hills I was brought forth;*

26 *While He had not yet made the earth and the fields,*

Nor the first dust of the world.

27 *"When He established the heavens, I was there,*

When He inscribed a circle on the face of the deep,

28 *When He made firm the skies above,*

When the springs of the deep became fixed,

29 *When He set for the sea its boundary*

So that the water would not transgress His command,

When He marked out the foundations of the earth;

30 *Then I was beside Him, as a master workman;*

And I was daily His delight, Rejoicing always before Him,

31*Rejoicing in the world, His earth, And having my delight in the sons of men.*

Jeremiah 10:12

It is He who made the earth by His power,

Who established the world by His wisdom;

And by His understanding He has stretched out the heavens.

God had a companion at creation – Wisdom. His wisdom was there at creation and it continues to be the dominant color in the tapestry of the created universe, despite the attempts of sin, suffering, and death to obscure it. Because of His wisdom:

- The earth is habitable for life as we know it

- The seasons occur by design
- The balance of nature is deliberate
- Atomic and sub-atomic particles operate in predictable ways
- Every star, moon, planet, galaxy, comet, and asteroid is there by design
- Things hold together
- We have food and water

In other words, we should look above at the skies and around at the earth, and we should marvel at the wisdom of God in designing and making it all. By His wisdom He made all of its amazing interactions and interdependencies. The Bible is clear: This is not a random world or universe. It is not a result of unguided, impersonal natural processes. When we take a breath, the air we breathe and the lungs that assimilate it into our bodies are there by God's wise design. Creation is the grand demonstration of God's intelligence, or more specifically, His wisdom.

His wisdom saturates every created thing, and no amount of sin can alter that. We look around at a chaotic world. We see decay, deformity, death, war, calamities, destruction, injustice, and disease, and we think, "That cannot have been created by God." We are right to think so. In original creation none of those things existed. They began when Adam sinned. The pristine world in which Adam was placed was a world of God's perfect wisdom and peace, but it was marred by death as soon as Adam ate the forbidden fruit. But even that catastrophic sin did not eradicate the evidences of divine wisdom in creation.

Those realities are the backdrop for God's redemption story. Just as sin and death began with a human and spread to all of creation, so redemption also began with a human and will spread to all of creation. According to the Scriptures, in wisdom God created the first Adam, who chose to violate God's wisdom and thereby brought sin and death to the world. Likewise in His wisdom and His love, God gave us the last Adam who brought righteousness, life, and redemption to the world. Both Adams reveal God's wisdom.

Psalm 104:24 comes at the culmination of the psalmist's recounting of the marvels of God's creation. The psalm has especially focused on God's providential care for His people and for animals. According to the psalm, it was by God's wisdom that He made all that exists. In wisdom:

- He made the land masses stable, vv. 5-9
- He provided food to support life, vv. 14-15, 21, 27
- He established day and night and the seasons, vv. 19-20
- He made rain and rivers for fresh water, vv. 10-13
- He gave people productive work, the ability to explore, and the skills to subdue, not abuse, the earth, v. 23
- He made it possible for His creatures to procreate, v. 30

This entire interdependent ecosystem was designed and created in wisdom by God; no other explanation is needed. Verse 24 does not say, "In wisdom You directed it all," but "In wisdom You have made them all [i.e., all the works of creation]." Life on this planet is possible only because God wisely designed and made everything, and it all points to one overarching purpose, the glory of God – *"Let the glory of the LORD endure forever,"* Psalm 104:31.

Psalm 136 is interesting because of the intertwining of the phrase "For His lovingkindness is everlasting" with all of the statements about God's creative work. Most of the psalm is a summary of God's goodness toward Israel. Interestingly, however, the psalmist did not begin with Abraham, Moses or the exodus, but with creation. Verses 1-4 are introductory exhortations to give thanks to the One who does great things. Then in verse 5, the psalm turns toward creation and notes that God made it "with skill." The word "skill" is also translated "wisdom" throughout the Old Testament. That is what wisdom is, the skillful application of knowledge.

In Psalm 136:5, we are told that everything in the heavens, including the sun and moon, was skillfully made by the Lord. God's hand, not a Big Bang, put all heavenly bodies exactly where He intended, including their complex motions in space. Dry land and the seas are separated according to God's skillful design. And the truly magnificent thing is this: This is not just a cold, hard universe made up of energy and matter, but the entire universe is saturated with the eternal lovingkindness of God. Therefore, we need not be frightened by the enormity of the heavens or by powerful geophysical forces, because it is all designed by God, made by Him, sustained by Him, and controlled by Him. He started it all with skill and maintains it all with love. For example, we might be amazed, even a little frightened, by the idea of a jumbo-jet becoming airborne, but we are comforted by knowing that it is in the control of a highly trained, capable and experienced pilot and crew. Similarly we are comforted as we contemplate the powerful jumbo-universe because it is not only piloted by the infinite and wise God, but it is also made by Him.

That God designed and made everything with wisdom is repeated in Proverbs 3:19, Jeremiah 10:12, and other passages. It is elaborated in Proverbs 8:22-31 where wisdom is personified as God's coworker in the creation of the heavens and the earth.

The implications of these passages are huge –

First, they provide the basis for scientific exploration and analysis. Because all things were made wisely, not randomly or sloppily, we can explore the physical world and heavens, confident that we are on the trail of God's wisdom.

Second, we need not fear that the "laws" of nature will arbitrarily and randomly change. God's wisdom and love are everlasting, so the things that He made in wisdom will remain as they were created. Clearly, living things grow and go through changes, but monkeys do not morph into cucumbers, rocks do not become poodles, air does not turn into acid, and humans do not change into turtles.

Third, despite the potentially frightening power of the earth's natural forces, we can take comfort in the fact that it is all made skillfully and lovingly by our Creator. Because our world is terminally broken and has been since Adam and Eve ate the forbidden fruit, bad things happen. But that does not erase the wisdom, power, and love of the Creator and Sustainer. The awfulness of sin, death, and calamities is the result of humans shunning God and His wisdom. But He has not abandoned us. He is saving, redeeming, regenerating, forgiving, and transforming us. He is a powerful yet gentle Shepherd, and even in the midst of suffering, His wise, kind purposes are always being accomplished in our lives. We really need to remember that.

RESPOND TO IT

1. When you look up into the heavens and look around at the world, describe the evidences of God's wisdom that you see?

2. How can we believe that God made everything with wisdom when so much is flawed and corrupted?

3. How do we, who are made in the image of God, reflect His wisdom?

27
THE CREATOR
FOUNDER

*Creation matters because it identifies
God as the earth's founder.*

Psalm 24:1-2

*1The earth is the LORD's, and all it contains,
The world, and those who dwell in it.
2For He has founded it upon the seas
And established it upon the rivers.*

Psalm 89:11

*The heavens are Yours, the earth also is Yours;
The world and all it contains, You have founded them.*

Psalm 104:5

*He established the earth upon its foundations,
So that it will not totter forever and ever.*

Job 38:4

*"Where were you when I laid the foundation of the earth?
Tell Me, if you have understanding,*

God owns us, the world, and everything in the heavens. He owns it all because He founded it all.

We have a tendency to see God's lordship as disconnected from the doctrine of creation. We need to be clear about this: The fact that He is Lord is rooted in the fact that He is Creator. The two are inseparable. For some, it's almost as if they think of God as discovering earth one day a long time ago and deciding to take over. Others seem to think of Him as having had a cooperative arrangement with the forces of nature, and together they formed the earth, the heavens, and everything in them, so they are co-founders, but God assumed full lordship once everything was made. Other people just don't know where the earth came from, but somehow believe there is a God who oversees it all. Then, of course, many others believe that there is a Creator God who is Lord over His creation.

Generally, Christians believe that God is the ultimate Lord of everything. But if we are vague in our belief that God is the Founder of the world, we will inevitably be vague in our confidence in His lordship. If we think that humans, the earth, and the heavens exist through a cooperative God-plus-something-else arrangement, then we will have difficulty believing that God has ultimate authority over life and circumstances here on earth. On the other hand, if we are convinced that He is the Founder-Owner of the heavens and the earth, then we ought to have no problem believing in His lordship over all, even if it takes our emotions a while to catch up. We can have total confidence that we are in His trustworthy loving care.

If we are not rock solid in that belief, the next trial that comes along might easily unsettle our faith and psychological equilibrium. Even small annoyances can derail our trust in Him. Isaiah 51:12-13 talks to this point:

12 *I, even I, am He who comforts you. Who are you that you are afraid of man who dies and of the son of man who is made like grass, 13 That you have forgotten the LORD your Maker, Who stretched out the heavens and laid the foundations of the earth, that you fear continually all day long because of the fury of the oppressor, as he makes ready to destroy? But where is the fury of the oppressor?"*

However, if we really believe that He is the Founder-Owner, we will affirm together with the words of Psalm 95:6-7:

6 Come, let us worship and bow down, Let us kneel before the LORD our Maker 7 For He is our God, And we are the people of His pasture and the sheep of His hand.

There is another aspect to the biblical teaching that the Lord is the Founder of the earth. It has to do with the stability that He has built into the world, making it a habitable place for humans, animals, and all other life-forms. Looking at this from the flip side, we do not reside in a world that developed randomly and is subject to enormous changes at any time, up to and including extinction. Once something is "established" or "founded," it is completed and meant to endure. For example, the United States was "founded" in the late 18th century and endures to this day. Likewise, the entirety of creation was God's work from start to finish. He established it, and it endures. He was its "founding Father." Therefore, it is more stable than any nation or organization.

Living on this planet, we take some things for granted. One of those things is that the earth is not hurtling randomly through space. Enormous physical and astrophysical forces keep the earth spinning reliably on its axis and orbiting consistently around the sun.

The word "foundation" in the verses above does not require a literalistic physical interpretation. In the original Hebrew and Greek of the Bible, the word is used both figuratively and literally in both the Old and New Testaments. For example, Psalm 97:2 says: *"Clouds and thick darkness surround Him; Righteousness and justice are the foundation of His throne."* We also see the figurative use in 1 Timothy 6:19: *storing up for themselves the treasure of a good foundation for the future, so that they may take hold of that which is life indeed.* In Psalm 104:5, the verb form of the word "established" means "fixed firmly." Hence, we can reasonably read this verse as saying that the earth is firmly fixed on a foundation of physical forces that keep it from "tottering."

Countless things are "established" – countries, programs, buildings, organizations, constitutions, pacts, etc. They all have certain things in common – they are planned, drawn up, developed, approved, and put to their intended use. The completion of their creation is also the beginning of their intended purpose. Psalm 104 highlights some of the things that the Lord does in the established earth, such as providing food and water for all living things, but there is no more there is no more establishing going on. That phase of earth history is complete.

Because we trust the Creator, that He laid the foundation of the earth once and for all, we do not need to worry that maybe everything will unexpectedly fly apart or be destroyed, until, of course, the day when the Lord Himself brings everything to a close. Most people do not go through life worrying that each day the world may suddenly come to a climactic end, but perhaps they ought to worry about that if they do not believe that the eternal God founded it and holds it together.

As we observe this established world and its place in space, we can be assured that the foundation is secure, not so much because of the laws of physics and astrophysics, but because of divine design and the assurances God has given us. This is a much bigger issue than mere science. It is all about the Creator – who He is and how He works.

RESPOND TO IT

1. Agree/Disagree: "If we are vague in our belief that God is the Founder of the world, we will be vague in our confidence in His lordship."

2. How can we find comfort in our distresses by understanding that God is the Founder?

3. To what extent do you believe that God is actually responsible for keeping the earth spinning steadily on its axis and revolving consistently around the sun?

28
THE CREATOR
CONTRA IDOLS

Creation matters because we become
idolaters if we do not believe it.

An idol is something other than Jesus Christ that has central place in our lives. We err if we think of them merely as an Old Testament problem, such as golden calves, carvings of false gods, or other ancient objects of pagan worship. They are also a current and present danger to American Christians, and we unfortunately and unwittingly embrace many idols. It is not just sinful things that can be defined as idols, but even many good things can become idols – houses, cars, success, family, big exciting churches, sports, careers, health, patriotism, sex, respectability, science, medicine, the economy, entertainment, influence, security, safety, politics, power, relevance, coolness, and the list goes on. On their own, each of these is not necessarily an idol, but they become idols when we stop seeing them as gifts from the triune God and start giving them priority over Him in our minds, hearts, and lifestyles. One guard, perhaps the primary guard, against indulging in idolatry is not just worshiping God, but worshiping the Creator God.

Psalm 96:5
For all the gods of the peoples are idols,
But the LORD made the heavens.

Isaiah 43:1, 7, 10-13

1*But now, thus says the Lord, your Creator, O Jacob,*
And He who formed you, O Israel...
7*"Everyone who is called by My name,*
And whom I have created for My glory,
Whom I have formed, even whom I have made."

10*"You are My witnesses," declares the Lord,*
"And My servant whom I have chosen,
So that you may know and believe Me
And understand that I am He.
Before Me there was no God formed,
And there will be none after Me.
11*"I, even I, am the Lord,*
And there is no savior besides Me.
12*"It is I who have declared and saved and proclaimed,*
And there was no strange god among you;
So you are My witnesses," declares the Lord,
"And I am God
13*"Even from eternity I am He,*
And there is none who can deliver out of My hand;
I act and who can reverse it?"

1 Corinthians 8:5-6

5 For even if there are so-called gods whether in heaven or on earth, as indeed there are many gods and many lords, 6 yet for us there is but one God, the Father, from whom are all things and we exist for Him; and one Lord, Jesus Christ, by whom are all things, and we exist through Him.

No matter how much good Bible teaching we get, we can still become idolaters. In fact, we almost can't help ourselves from falling into idolatry, to one degree or another. It creeps into our lives as our sinful hearts neglect to thank God for His gifts and we become absorbed with the gifts themselves. The problem is reinforced because we are surrounded by a culture for which many kinds of idolatry are completely acceptable. We try to apply biblical truths to our lives, but the lure of idolatry is subtle and pernicious.

The trouble begins when we separate, deliberately or unconsciously, the Christian part of our lives from the other parts of our lives, when we come to a point where Jesus is important to us but not supreme, when the Bible intersects our lives rather than defines our lives. When we neglect to filter our choices, opinions, and desires through the Word of God, we open the door for wrong thinking to enter our minds. One symptom of that wrong thinking is an inordinate love for something in creation. Whatever that thing is, even if it is a good thing, it has become an idol.

An idol is any object, any idea, any person, any group, any activity, any goal, or any other created thing that does the following:

- It is the dominant source of comfort, purpose, meaning, and direction for our lives.
- It is the primary source of satisfaction, joy, and/or pleasure for our lives.
- It defines who we are.
- It is something we daydream about, sacrifice for, and devote ourselves to.
- It makes Jesus Christ important, but secondary, in our lives.

Anything can become an idol. Gratitude is one antidote against idolatry. We can prevent something from becoming an idol if we view it with gratitude as a gift from the Lord, try to be godly stewards of it, and place it in subjection to Jesus Christ. As I noted above, there is a long list of things, some clearly sinful but others good, that can displace Christ from His primary place in our lives. And, there are many contributing causes for this, but one of the major ones is our forgetfulness, or ignorance, of the fact that God is the Creator.

If we look at the world and skies above and are overwhelmed with the majesty, power, and wisdom of the Creator, we are less likely to fall into some sort of idolatry. We do not worship a vague, remote, detached deity. Our God is Jesus Christ, through whom everything exists and holds together. He has power and authority over all creation. But if our field of vision narrows so that we see only the creation, to the diminishment of the Creator, our eventual idolatry is practically assured.

It is easy to see how our thinking can cascade into idolatry – We start by observing something in the heavens or on earth that captures our attention; we become absorbed with it; then we come to rely on it, dream about it, and talk about it; before long we are willing to sacrifice for it in terms of our time, money, and energies; eventually we begin to define ourselves in terms of it, making it the sole orienting feature of our lives. At that point we have become full-blown idolaters. Christians are just as susceptible to this as non-Christians.

Psalm 96:5 cinches the connection between worshiping either the Creator or idols. It lays out only two options: one, recognize the majesty and splendor of the Creator God, or two, embrace idols. Ultimately those are the only two options; there is no middle ground. The Isaiah 43 passage reinforces this truth and points us to the path away from idolatry, namely to focus on one important truth about God, namely that He is the Creator. The passage begins with the assertion that the Lord created us, and He did so for His glory. He made us and the world in which we reside. He is the one and only eternal God. He alone is the Savior. Only He, not the universe, is eternal.

Unless we can read passages like Isaiah 43 and say to ourselves, "This stuff is actually true; God really is our Creator," we are on track to some sort of idolatry.

RESPOND TO IT

1. Agree/Disagree: The guard against indulging in idolatry is not just worship of God, but worship of God as Creator.

2. Agree/Disagree: Idolatry is a real possibility for you.

3. What are some things that are potential idols for us? How does understanding that God is the Creator help us avoid the pitfall of idolatry? How does gratitude help?

FOUNDATION

Creation does not stand in isolation from other teachings in Scripture. In fact, it is the foundation for many of them. In studies 29-34 we will examine several biblical teachings that rely on creation.

29
FOUNDATION
THE INCARNATION

Creation matters because it explains Christ's incarnation.

John 1:1-3, 14

1In the beginning was the Word, and the Word was with God, and the Word was God. 2He was in the beginning with God. 3All things came into being through Him, and apart from Him nothing came into being that has come into being.

14And the Word became flesh, and dwelt among us, and we saw His glory, glory as of the only begotten from the Father, full of grace and truth.

Colossians 1:15-17

15He is the image of the invisible God, the firstborn of all creation. 16For by Him all things were created, both in the heavens and on earth, visible and invisible, whether thrones or dominions or rulers or authorities—all things have been created through Him and for Him. 17He is before all things, and in Him all things hold together.

By "incarnation" we mean that the pre-existing Son of God took on human flesh without ceasing to be fully and truly divine. Jesus Christ was born in Bethlehem to His mother Mary, but He had existed eternally prior to that as the second person of the Trinity. He was not a mere mortal who acquired deity at some point after His birth, but was the eternal God who became a man.

Jesus Christ is the God who created everything. He came into the world that He created, in the form of a human being, a form that He had created in His own image. He did not come as a spirit, or as a nebulous divine influence, or as an alien, or as an animal. He came as a real man, in real time. In the incarnation, the Lord affirmed two creation truths:

- One, this is His planet, not someone or something else's.
- Two, the human body is His intentional creation, not the product of random naturalistic processes.

This planet is the purposeful creation of Jesus Christ, God the Son. Humans are His purposeful creation, and in fact we are His highest creation, because only we are made in His image. Therefore, when He came, He entered into a place that He made and owns, in a form that He made, the highest life-form in all creation.

If this world were not His creation and if we were not made in His image, the incarnation would be a mere accommodation of an outside deity pulling off an impressive feat, but always an outsider. But instead, creation and the incarnation are inextricably linked. Christ came on a redeeming mission to His own creation to reveal and restore us to the infinitely loving Creator God. He came, not as an alien stranger, but as one of us. He did not just take on a convenient form that happened to have evolved on this planet, but a form designed and made by Him, so He knows everything about us. This world is His creation, so He also knows everything about it. He did not appear in someone else's property but in the place of His own design and making. This is His turf and we are His people

We are His creation residing in a world He created. Therefore, in the incarnation God was participating in what He made, and He did so in the only form made in His image. He came as part of creation, not as an outsider to it. The human body was not strange to Him; He was at home in it just as He was at home in the world He created.

RESPOND TO IT

1. Discuss the implications of Jesus coming to earth as a human being rather than in some other form.

2. Some Christians think that the Son of God came into existence when Jesus was born to Mary, but in actuality He is the pre-existing God who created everything. Is this truth new to you? Discuss its implications.

3. How does the incarnation affect you?

30
FOUNDATION
SALVATION

Creation matters because it is the explanation for Christians being a new creation in Christ.

2 Corinthians 5:14-21

14For the love of Christ controls us, having concluded this, that one died for all, therefore all died; 15and He died for all, so that they who live might no longer live for themselves, but for Him who died and rose again on their behalf.

16Therefore from now on we recognize no one according to the flesh; even though we have known Christ according to the flesh, yet now we know Him in this way no longer. 17Therefore if anyone is in Christ, he is a new creature [lit: new creation]; the old things passed away; behold, new things have come. 18Now all these things are from God, who reconciled us to Himself through Christ and gave us the ministry of reconciliation, 19namely, that God was in Christ reconciling the world to Himself, not counting their trespasses against them, and He has committed to us the word of reconciliation.

20Therefore, we are ambassadors for Christ, as though God were making an appeal through us; we beg you on behalf of Christ, be reconciled to God. 21He made Him who knew no sin to be sin on our behalf, so that we might become the righteousness of God in Him.

When God created the heavens and earth, He did not merely take existing stuff and creatively refashion it. Rather, He spoke, and where previously nothing existed, an entire universe sprang into being. He did not just take control of an already-existing cosmos; He made the cosmos. Creating is what He does.

In theological terms, God created ex nihilo – out of nothing. That is the story of Genesis 1-2. That is also the model for what happens when a person becomes a Christian.

As the apostle Paul described salvation in 2 Corinthians 5:14-21, he used creation as the model for what happens when God saves us. In verse 17, when he refers to a "new creation," he is pointing us to two significant aspects of salvation:

First, it is instantaneous, not gradual.

Second, God is an active, not a passive, deity.

Regarding the first aspect of salvation in 2 Corinthians 5:17, a person does not slowly grow into becoming a Christian. Rather, in a moment of time a person goes from being a non-Christian to being a Christian. We may go through a process leading us to the point of salvation, and following our salvation we experience a life-long process of transformation, but when salvation happens, it is immediate and total, just as original creation was.

We, as Christians, are not just fixed-up or evolved versions of our old selves; we are brand new beings with a new nature that is sprung out of nothing. We are a new creation, not a makeover, not a rework. That is what God does for each person who puts his or her faith in Jesus Christ. At original creation something brand new, namely the universe, sprang into existence. As a new creation, whether we feel it or not, we become totally new beings when we trust in Christ. Our old self died (v. 14) and something totally new exists in its place. Colossians 3:3 says: *For you have died and your life is hidden with Christ in God.* Creation explains this reality.

Paul reinforces this idea of salvation being a matter of a new creation rather than a redo. In Galatians 6:14-15 he says: *14But may it never be that I would boast, except in the cross of our Lord Jesus Christ, through which the world has been crucified to me, and I to the world. 15For neither is circumcision anything, nor uncircumcision, but a new creation.* His point was that religion does not make a person a Christian, only "a new creation" does. In fact, there is nothing we can do that will make us right with God, apart from being dead to the world and alive in Christ.

Something extraordinary happened when we became believers. We did more than become converts to Christianity, we became newly created beings. Something that did not exist previously now exists, namely a Christian self. This new self co-mingles with the prior self, but is not just an improved version of it. It exists alongside the prior self, but is separate from it; the new identifies with the prior, but is unequal to it; the new is influenced by the prior, but is independent of it.

We may or may not have felt this amazing creation happen, but each of us knew that something was different. The original creation of everything is the backdrop, the framework, the model for the new creation of a person who comes to know Christ.

The connection between creation and salvation was crucial in Paul's mind. In Ephesians 2:10 he wrote: *For we are His workmanship, created in Christ Jesus for good works, which God prepared beforehand so that we would walk in them.* Then later in 4:24, he elaborated on this idea when he wrote: *and put on the new self, which in the likeness of God has been created in righteousness and holiness of the truth.* There are books written on the subject of the "old self" and the "new self," but for the sake of the present discussion, there is one point that we need to be clear about. Specifically, just as original creation brought into existence instantaneously an entire universe, so salvation brings a new person into existence instantaneously.

This brings us to the second significant aspect of salvation described in 2 Corinthians 5:17, namely that God is not a passive deity, or to put it another way, He is an initiative-taking God. He took the initiative in creating the cosmos and everything in it. He took the initiative in revealing Himself, in providing a plan of salvation, in drawing us to Himself. He continues to take the initiative in transforming us into the likeness of Jesus Christ, and He will take the initiative in wrapping up earth history at the end of time. Despite appearances, the circumstances in our lives and in the world are the product of God's initiative.

Every time we see someone become a Christian, we should be reminded that we live in a world created by the Lord in a moment of time, and that He took the initiative to not only create the world but to make us a new creation.

RESPOND TO IT

1. "We, as Christians, are not just fixed-up or evolved versions of our old selves; we are brand new beings with a new nature that is sprung out of nothing. We are a new creation, not a makeover, not a rework." Is that how you see it?

2. The statement is made in this study: "This new self co-mingles with the prior self, but is not just an improved version of it. It exists alongside the prior self, but is separate from it; the new identifies with the prior, but is unequal to it; the new is influenced by the prior, but is independent of it." Try to think of ways to describe the fact that we are a new creation rather than a fixed-up version of our old selves, while yet our old self continues to influence us.

31
FOUNDATION
PRAYER

Creation matters because it is a basis for prayer.

2 Kings 19:15

Hezekiah prayed before the Lord and said, "O Lord, the God of Israel, who are enthroned above the cherubim, You are the God, You alone, of all the kingdoms of the earth. You have made heaven and earth.

Acts 4:24

And when they heard this, they lifted their voices to God with one accord and said, "O Lord, it is You who made the heaven and the earth and the sea, and all that is in them,

Nehemiah 9:5b-6

5"...Oh may Your glorious name be blessed
And exalted above all blessing and praise!
6"You alone are the Lord.
You have made the heavens,
The heaven of heavens with all their host,
The earth and all that is on it,
The seas and all that is in them.
You give life to all of them
And the heavenly host bows down before You.

Psalm 33:6-9

6By the word of the LORD the heavens were made,
And by the breath of His mouth all their host.
7He gathers the waters of the sea together as a heap;
He lays up the deeps in storehouses.
8Let all the earth fear the LORD;
Let all the inhabitants of the world stand in awe of Him.
9For He spoke, and it was done;
He commanded, and it stood fast.

Prayers begin in many ways in Scripture, often with an expression of praise for some aspect of who God is. The beginning of the prayer is never unrelated to the rest of the prayer, but rather is purposefully tied to the requests that will follow. Therefore, in several instances when creation is mentioned in the opening words of a prayer, it is for specific reasons.

Reason #1: Protection.

We have already looked at Acts 4:24 in an earlier section, but there is still a little more insight that we can gain from this verse. The apostles were facing an immediate threat, the gospel was under attack, and persecution had already begun. In today's culture of increasing hostility toward Christians, this is a very important prayer for us to remember. Of all the possible things for which they could praise God, why did the apostles start their prayer by praising God as the Creator? As we have observed in the prior study of this verse, if God is the Creator, then He is more powerful than anything or anyone. Therefore, by acknowledging God as Creator, the apostles knew that they had hope, comfort, and confidence in the face of imminent opposition and suffering. If we are anxious and fretful about impending persecution, maybe our problem is that we really do not believe that God is the Maker of the heavens and earth. If we take away the doctrine of creation, things in this life become uncertain, distressing, and even terrifying. Our confidence in His power and protection is based on the fact that He is Creator.

This was one of the first things King Hezekiah prayed when the nation faced a potential violent overthrow by the Assyrian king Sennacherib, as recorded in 2 Kings 19:15. Hezekiah knew that the Lord was more powerful than all supernatural spirits and all nations of the earth, because He had created them. God is just as sovereign over the opposition as He is sovereign over the lives of His beloved people because He created both.

A thing created cannot be greater than its creator. Similarly, a thing created is sustained by its creator, not vice versa. Contrary to the deists who see God as a divine watchmaker who abandoned the watch after He wound it up, the Scriptures affirm that God is the ongoing sustainer and overseer of His creation. Therefore creation matters because it is the basis of our confidence that God is actually in control. It should be the default thought about God in our minds when opposition against us is on the rise.

Reason #2: Confession.

Not every prayer of confession refers to creation, but a very long and important one in Nehemiah does. The reference to God as the Maker of the heavens and earth at the very beginning of the prayer of confession tells us some things to keep in mind as we confess our sins to the Lord. One, we need to remember that we reside as created beings in a created world, and God designed us to live a certain way according to His rules on this earth. But we violate His ways continually, so we need to repent not only because He is holy, righteous, and just, but also because He is the Creator. The creation account in Genesis 1-2 has never been superseded, updated, or replaced. It should still be the backdrop for our prayers of confession. Two, when we sin, we are not merely violating a moral code, but we are violating the very essence of creation itself. God's precepts and laws are not arbitrary rules that He imposed on humans as we populated the earth. Rather, they are expressions of the Creator woven into the fabric of creation. Nehemiah knew that sin was contrary to creation as well as to God's laws. When we sin, we are disrupting creation, to one degree or another.

This is an important reason why creation matters – it is the basis of our confessions to God. He made the earth and everything in it. As the Creator, He also established the rules and guidelines for how we should live. Therefore, creation should be the default thought about God in our minds when we confess our sins to Him.

Reason #3: Praise.

God's people have always gathered regularly to worship Him. Worship is an end in itself, not a means to an end. I heard an enthusiastic pastor recently exclaim on a Sunday morning, "This is more than worship! This is an experience of God!" He was very wrong. He was leading his congregation astray by telling them that there is something beyond worship, namely experience. He was wrong because he was taking the focus off the God being worshiped and placing it on the worshipers. In true worship, we lose our self-consciousness and become absorbed with the glory of the triune God. For example, a football fan who is cheering wildly when his team wins the Super Bowl is so caught up in the team's victory that he is nearly unaware of his own self and is totally wrapped up in the accomplishments of the team. Let's call it the Super-Bowl-Effect.

The Psalms have been used in worship for centuries, and they include many references to God as Creator. Truly understanding what God did at creation should produce something like the Super-Bowl-Effect. We should have that response when we read passages like Psalm 33:6-9. God spoke...and a full-blown universe sprang into being. A human being cannot speak anything into being, but words from God's mouth created everything. That is the power of God's word, and it should draw us outside ourselves in awe and worship.

Think of fantasy stories in which an innocent-looking object turns out to have enormous power. Maybe it is the "one ring to rule them all" in the "Lord of the Rings." Maybe it is a magic mirror in a fairy tale that reveals far more than a reflection. People invent such stories because deep within us is the awareness that some things in reality have far more power than they appear to have on the surface. The Bible is one of those things. Just as God's words created the heavens, earth and all that is in them, so God's Word, the Scriptures, has that same power to create new life and transform us.

This is another reason why creation matters – it is the basis of our praise as we stand in awe of the Creator God. Therefore, it should be our default thought as we consider His works, such as when we watch a sunset, see a newborn baby, or gaze at a majestic mountain range. Our wonder-working God is deserving of our praise and worship.

RESPOND TO IT

1. How can we incorporate creation into our prayers when we:

    o confess sins

    o pray for protection

    o praise Him

    o ask for wisdom

    o request solutions for difficulties?

2. To what extent do you agree with the statement: "[W]hen we sin, we are not merely violating a moral code, but we are violating the very essence of creation itself"?

32
FOUNDATION
THE OMNI-GOD

Creation matters because it reveals God's omniscience, omnipotence, and omnipresence.

Psalm 33:15

He who fashions the hearts of them all,
He who understands all their works

Jeremiah 32:17

'Ah LORD God! Behold, You have made the heavens and the earth by Your great power and by Your outstretched arm! Nothing is too difficult for You,

Psalm 139:7-10, 13-16

7Where can I go from Your Spirit?
Or where can I flee from Your presence?
8If I ascend to heaven, You are there;
If I make my bed in Sheol, behold, You are there.
9If I take the wings of the dawn,
If I dwell in the remotest part of the sea,
10Even there Your hand will lead me,
And Your right hand will lay hold of me.

13For You formed my inward parts;
You wove me in my mother's womb.

*14I will give thanks to You, for I am fearfully and
wonderfully made;*
Wonderful are Your works,
And my soul knows it very well.
15My frame was not hidden from You,
When I was made in secret,
And skillfully wrought in the depths of the earth;
16Your eyes have seen my unformed substance;
And in Your book were all written
The days that were ordained for me,
When as yet there was not one of them.

These verses reveal three important "omni" characteristics of the Lord. Each of these characteristics of the Lord is tied to creation.

- God is omniscient – He knows everything.
- God is omnipotent – He can do anything.
- God is omnipresent – He is everywhere.

God knows everything. That seems fairly intuitive to most of us. He knows everything about science, math, psychology, and languages; He knows everything that ever happened, is happening, and will happen; He knows everything about every planet and star in the skies; He knows everything about us. We can find plenty of verses that affirm these truths. Psalm 33:15 presents us with a formal explanation for His omniscience – He made us. Therefore He knows everything about us. He is not omniscient because that is what gods are supposed to be; rather He is omniscient because He made everything, including us. An artist knows every brush stroke in a painting; a carpenter knows every square inch of a piece of furniture. Likewise, God knows everything about us.

God can do anything. His power is limitless. That also seems fairly intuitive to most of us, but sometimes we harbor doubts about it.

Maybe we agree theologically, but we are unsure practically. We would just like to see more evidence of His power. The problem, however, is not that He holds back His power, but that we are defining on our own terms how it should be manifested. We are troubled that He does not stop terrorists or heal loved ones who have terminal illnesses. We have conflicts or experience bad things, and feel like praying, "Lord, look what happened while You were away! Where have You been?" We would like for Him to show His power a little more in the ways that would satisfy us. But that's not the way it works. He has told us often where to look to see His power.

The Lord starts by pointing to creation. Right there is where we see God's power. Because He could create a universe with all its life forms, we know He can do anything – *Ah LORD God! Behold, You have made the heavens and the earth by Your great power and by Your outstretched arm! Nothing is too difficult for You,* Jeremiah 32:17. Whether or not He chooses to exercise His power in a way that we would like Him to is beside the point. God has both power and a will, so He decides when, where, and how He will demonstrate it. We need to remember, He did not have to create anything; He did so in keeping with His own will, in His own timing, and in His own way. He did not acquire the universe or step in as a surrogate God, because if that were so, then there would be another Being or Force, probably greater than Him, that made everything. Rather He is that ultimate Creator. If He is not, then we live in an uncertain world where maybe the original creator could show up at any time, thump the Lord, and carry out whatever plan he has, perhaps a malicious one. But if the Lord is the Creator, as the Bible claims, there is no power superior to Him, and He is good. Everything and everybody is created by Him and under His authority. We rely on that fact, whether or not He acts according to our will. Our prayer should always be, "Thy will be done."

God is everywhere. From the bottom of the ocean to the most distant galaxy, God is there. In English Composition courses we learned the word "synecdoche," which is a literary device for using a part of something to represent the whole. For example, if we see a friend's new car and say something like, "Nice wheels," we are using a synecdoche. The wheels, as a small part of the car, represent the whole car. In Psalm 139 David used a synecdoche to connect God's creation to His omnipresence, specifically he used himself as a synecdoche, a representative of the whole human race. All of us, like David, were formed by the Lord. Not only did God create Adam and Eve uniquely, but each person since then is specially formed by God. Beginning with conception, the development of our bodies and souls is purposely and personally overseen by God. He established the human reproductive, development, and growth processes when He made Adam and Eve, but He did not stop there. Just as He superintends everything else, He superintends the development and growth of each person from conception onward.

The Psalm carries the synecdoche a step further. Representing humanity, David asserted that we could not go anywhere in the universe and get away from God. The universe is far too small to contain God, so there is no escaping from Him. There are no secret places, no privacy...anywhere. Wherever we go, whatever we do, the Lord is there. He is watching, not from a distance, but up-close and personal, all the time. The conclusion of this thought is not so much theological or scientific, but moral –

Psalm 139:23-24
23 Search me, O God, and know my heart;
Try me and know my anxious thoughts;
24 And see if there be any hurtful way in me,
And lead me in the everlasting way.

RESPOND TO IT

1. Discuss the implications: "He continues to superintend the development and growth of each person from conception onward."

2. Discuss the implications of:
   - God's omnipresence on our morality.
   - God's omniscience on our thought-life.
   - God's omnipotence on how we go through difficulties.

3. Discuss what might happen in our lives if we pray the prayer of David in Psalm 139:23-24.

33
FOUNDATION
JUSTICE

Creation matters because it is the basis for justice.

Job 34:19
Who shows no partiality to princes
Nor regards the rich above the poor,
For they all are the work of His hands?

Psalm 33:5-6
5He loves righteousness and justice;
The earth is full of the lovingkindness of the LORD.
6By the word of the LORD the heavens were made,
And by the breath of His mouth all their host.

Psalm 146:5-7
5How blessed is he whose help is the God of Jacob,
Whose hope is in the LORD his God,
6Who made heaven and earth,
The sea and all that is in them;
Who keeps faith forever;
7Who executes justice for the oppressed;
Who gives food to the hungry.
The LORD sets the prisoners free.

Proverbs 14:31

He who oppresses the poor taunts his Maker,
But he who is gracious to the needy honors Him.

Ecclesiastes 7:29

Behold, I have found only this, that God made men upright, but they have sought out many devices."

"That's just not fair!" is a familiar cry of children toward their parents, students in the classroom, and adults about their bosses. There is something inside each of us that craves for justice. In the Bible "justice" means more than just playing fair. Its root word in Hebrew is also frequently translated "righteousness." Therefore, it means to do what is right, and to do it the right way. Expanding on that, it includes avoiding partiality, and instead showing kindness, love and respect for all people.

A just person is generous to the less fortunate, is not devious or treacherous, is honest, and lives by faith in God rather than by his or her own feelings and wisdom. All of these things can be derived from the above verses. A significant common thread is this: All these aspects of justice go back to God as the Creator. That explains the universal innate sense of justice that we all have.

We should be just because God made us in His image and He is just. He never shows partiality to anyone because He made everyone and cares for all people equally. He is not impressed by successful, influential people; neither is He uncaring about unimpressive people. In God's eyes all lives matter. We are not all equally gifted or skilled, but we are all equally created in God's image and loved by Him. We all are equally required to be just and righteous. Those to whom He has granted special gifts, skills, and abilities have a responsibility to use them to serve and be gracious to others and make people's lives better. A person who ignores or mocks the less fortunate is mocking God. This is not a small matter; it goes right to the supreme court of heaven. Generosity and kindness are expressions of the justice that God requires of all of us. The Creator acts this way, and He wants those who are created in His image, which means everyone, to act this way also.

Another window into justice is in Ecclesiastes 7:29. The word justice is not found there, but the concept is. The verse looks back to the original humans who God created, Adam and Eve, and states a simple truth about them: God made them, and He made them to be upright – spiritually committed to the Lord, morally pure, and just. But in this one verse the whole calamitous fall of the human race is summarized. Instead of remaining upright as God created us to be, we have sought out other ways. Those many devices are all the ways we have figured out how to do things our own way, by being unrighteous, self-indulgent, and unjust toward others. Hence, injustice is not just a moral issue, it is a creation issue; specifically it is contra-creation.

Creation matters because it is the basis and safeguard for the idea of justice. Justice did not arise as a later idea sometime after the earth was created, but it is woven into the fabric of creation and into the souls of each person, for we are each created in the image of the just God.

RESPOND TO IT

1. How have you seen justice, or its absence, recently?

2. Why is justice a matter of creation and not just a social/moral issue?

3. How can each of us show justice in our daily lives?

34
FOUNDATION
SECURITY
Creation matters because it is why we are secure.

Romans 8:38-39

38For I am convinced that neither death, nor life, nor angels, nor principalities, nor things present, nor things to come, nor powers, 39nor height, nor depth, nor any other created thing, will be able to separate us from the love of God, which is in Christ Jesus our Lord.

We find great comfort in these verses, and rightly so. They come at the conclusion of a passage where Paul has been telling us all that God has done, still does, and will do for us through Jesus Christ. He assures us of the Lord's sovereign, eternal love and our security in Him. As we savor those truths, we may pass right over some significant words in verse 39: "nor any other created thing." Everything that Paul has just mentioned in these two verses was created by God, and there are other created things which did not even get on the list.

Creation is the frame around the picture Paul paints in verses 38-39. Interestingly, even death is on the list of created things, as strange as that may sound. Recall that prior to Adam's fall in the pristine perfect environment of the Garden, God already warned him about death: "In the day that you eat from it, you will surely die." Death was not a feature of original creation, and yet it was already established by God, ready to be unleashed if and when Adam would choose to disobey the Lord. It is an intruder, but not a surprise to God. Death's source is the Creator God, but unlike everything else in original creation, it is not "good." It came after creation, but was imposed upon it by the Lord Himself in response to Adam's sin. It was His curse for disobedience, so it is in fact, an "enemy," humanity's greatest fear. But just as He imposed death upon the human race, He also obliterated it through Jesus Christ. He saved us from something of His own doing. By placing death first on his list, Paul is making the point that if death itself is incapable of separating us from God's love in Christ then neither can any other created thing do so.

Paul was very clear – Our security is not based on a general concept of God's strength and care, but on the specific concept of God's creation. There are no other gods, and there is nothing that God did not create, so we do not need to worry about some malevolent thing or being from outside creation snatching us out of God's hands. All of our problems originate within the context of God's created universe. And none of those problems is greater than the Creator's power to preserve us through Christ.

Things go badly, evil exists, and people suffer. These things were not intended when God created the world. They were and are the symptoms of broken creation, the consequences of our rejection of the Creator. All the bad that happens on earth occurs from within the scope of creation, never as an alien invasion from outside it or from a wicked independent competitor god. Once we understand that, we begin to understand the awesome significance of Jesus Christ and the security that is found in Him. Through Him, God created everything, rules everything, will conquer all His enemies, and keeps us secure in His loving care. Through Christ, He is redeeming us within the context of this created world. Nothing in all of creation can thwart that, and there is nothing outside creation that can intrude upon it. The only thing that exists outside creation is the triune God, and He acts on our behalf.

RESPOND TO IT

1. When Paul tells us about our security in Christ, why does he bring creation into the picture?

2. Discuss: "Our security is not based on a general concept of God's strength and care, but on the specific concept of God's creation."

3. How is knowing that death itself has its source in the Creator God a comfort in light of the Romans 8:38-39 passage?

ANTHROPOLOGY

Most colleges and universities offer courses in anthropology. The dictionary definition of "anthropology" is: the science that deals with the origins, physical and cultural development, biological characteristics, and social customs and beliefs of humankind. When we look at biblical anthropology, we are studying what the Bible says about these things. A secularist sees humans as the result of a long evolutionary process; a Christian sees humans as the direct creation of the infinite, personal, loving God. In studies 35-40 we look at several aspects of what and who we are in light of creation.

35

ANTHROPOLOGY
OUR ORIGIN

Creation matters because it is the explanation for Christians being a new creation in Christ.

The following verses teach us two important truths.

IMPORTANT TRUTH #1: WE CAN ALL TRACE OUR ANCESTRY BACK TO A LITERAL ADAM AND EVE.

Genesis 1:27-28

27God created man in His own image, in the image of God He created him; male and female He created them. 28God blessed them; and God said to them, "Be fruitful and multiply, and fill the earth, and subdue it; and rule over the fish of the sea and over the birds of the sky and over every living thing that moves on the earth."

Genesis 2:7

Then the LORD God formed man of dust from the ground, and breathed into his nostrils the breath of life; and man became a living being.

Luke 3:23, 38

23When He began His ministry, Jesus Himself was about thirty years of age, being, as was supposed, the son of Joseph, the son of Eli.....38the son of Enosh, the son of Seth, the son of Adam, the son of God.

1 Corinthians 15:45-47

45So also it is written, "The first man, Adam, became a living soul." The last Adam became a life-giving spirit. 46 However, the spiritual is not first, but the natural; then the spiritual. 47The first man is from the earth, earthy; the second man is from heaven.

IMPORTANT TRUTH #2: WE ARE ALL FASHIONED BY GOD IN OUR MOTHERS' WOMBS.

Psalm 119:73

Your hands made me and fashioned me;
Give me understanding, that I may learn Your commandments.

Psalm 139:13-15

13For You formed my inward parts;
You wove me in my mother's womb.

14I will give thanks to You, for I am fearfully and wonderfully made; Wonderful are Your works,
And my soul knows it very well.

15My frame was not hidden from You,
When I was made in secret,
And skillfully wrought in the depths of the earth;

Isaiah 44:2

Thus says the LORD who made you,
And formed you from the womb, who will help you,
'Do not fear, O Jacob My servant;
And you Jeshurun whom I have chosen.

Who were the original parents of the human race? When and where did they live? Secularists see these as yet-unanswered questions. Christians believe that the Bible answers them. Our starting point is the triune Creator God. If a person denies this, that person is denying a foundational truth of the Christian faith, a belief that is asserted in the Bible and has been affirmed by the church for twenty centuries. Together Christians should be able to say, "I believe in God the Father almighty, Maker of heaven and earth."

Starting with Genesis and continuing into the New Testament, the Scriptures affirm a literal Adam and Eve who existed within recorded history. Unlike all the animals which God spoke into existence, Adam was formed from the dust of the ground. He was not the offspring of any living creatures; he was from earth. Eve also had no parents; she was formed from Adam's rib. She is the one person in the history of the world who came from a man rather than from a woman. They became the original parents of every person on earth today. The genealogy of every person goes back to Adam and Eve. They must have lived in the not-too-distant past – thousands, not millions, of years ago. Otherwise the biblical genealogies would have no credibility.

Based on that starting point, the Scriptures affirm that each person is formed and fashioned by God from the moment of our conception in our mothers' wombs. This is not the same as the original creation of Adam and Eve, but it is derived from that. When God made Adam and Eve, He also built the human procreative process into them and, hence, into all their descendants. With Adam and Eve as the model, the Bible confidently says that we are all the work of God's hand. None of us is an accident.

The idea that God made us is fundamental to a biblical view of anthropology. Our identity lies in the fact that humans are the direct supernatural handiwork of a personal Creator. He made us from dust, not from other beings. Psalm 139:13-15, quoted above, is just as true of every human being on earth today as it was true of David.

The Christian relies on a fundamental truth:

Psalm 100:3
Know that the LORD Himself is God;
It is He who has made us, and not we ourselves;
We are His people and the sheep of His pasture.

RESPOND TO IT

1. Agree/Disagree: "The genealogy of every person goes back to Adam and Eve. They must have lived in the not-too-distant past – thousands, not millions, of years ago. Otherwise the biblical genealogies would have no credibility."

2. What are some implications of the fact that God fashions us while we are still in our mothers' wombs?

36
ANTHROPOLOGY
HEART AND SOUL

*Creation matters because it explains
the existence of our souls.*

Job 38:36
*"Who has put wisdom in the innermost being,
Or given understanding to the mind?*

Psalm 33:15
*He who fashions the hearts of them all,
He who understands all their works.*

Naturalistic explanations for our existence will always struggle to explain the origin of the immaterial part of us. Why do we feel? Why are we self-conscious? Why do we pray? Why do we have hopes, values, and ethics? Where did our ability to reason and understand come from? Why do we have a sense of purpose and self-worth? Why do we want to leave a legacy that will continue after we die? Secularists have developed intelligent, sophisticated responses to these questions, but they cannot adequately explain the nagging feeling we all have that we are something more than a complex arrangement of molecules. But, the problem is, if there is no transcendent Creator, our souls are merely the product of molecular interactions in our bodies.

The Bible teaches that human beings are an interwoven blend of material and immaterial. We have bodies and we have souls. They are neither totally separate nor totally united. Our souls – including our intellect, emotions, and wills – are linked to our brains, but are nonetheless also independent of our bodies. At physical conception an eternal soul is also conceived. Throughout our lives, our souls are indeed united to our bodies, but we are still aware that there is something more. The reason is that God placed wisdom and understanding – inclusive of our minds, emotions, and wills -- into us. Our ability to think, feel, and choose comes from Him, not just from the molecules in our brains, or from natural processes, or from cultural influences. Our minds are linked to, but not co-equal with, our brains.

Our souls, our inner selves, are a major part of what it means to be human, made in the image of God. Everything about us – our bodies, our sexuality, and our immaterial selves – are from God, reflective of God, and designed to enable us to know God. We should note that the Bible frequently talks about our bodies and our minds, but not about our brains. In fact, often, Paul contrasts our flesh and our minds. [1]

This needs to be emphasized: The entirety of a human being is made by God. He forms both our material and our immaterial parts. He links them at conception and keeps them linked throughout our lives. Simultaneously, He informs us that there is more to us than just our physical bodies. Deep inside us, we are all aware that we are not merely finite, physical mortals. That awareness is by design – God *"has also set eternity in their heart,"* Ecclesiastes 3:11. As mentioned above, this explains the sense we all have that there is something more, that this physical flesh is not all there is. Eventually He will unite our souls with a glorified body that will reside in His presence forever.

1, Consider such passages as Rom. 7:25, 8:5-7; Eph. 2:3; Phil. 3:4; and Col. 2:18.

RESPOND TO IT

1. Discuss: What is our soul?

2. In what ways is our soul linked to our bodies? How does this affect the way you understand our future eternal state?

37
ANTHROPOLOGY
Sexuality

Creation matters because it is the foundation for understanding our sexuality.

Genesis 1:27

God created man in His own image, in the image of God He created him; male and female He created them.

Matthew 19:4-6

4And He answered and said, "Have you not read that He who created them from the beginning made them male and female, 5and said, 'For this reason a man shall leave his father and mother and be joined to his wife, and the two shall become one flesh'? 6So they are no longer two, but one flesh. What therefore God has joined together, let no man separate."

Mark 10:6

But from the beginning of creation, God made them male and female.

1 Corinthians 11:8-12

8For man does not originate from woman, but woman from man; 9for indeed man was not created for the woman's sake, but woman for the man's sake. 10Therefore the woman ought to have a symbol of authority on her head, because of the angels. 11However, in the Lord, neither is woman independent of man, nor is man independent of woman. 12For as the woman originates from the man, so also the man has his birth through the woman; and all things originate from God.

The environment in the United States today is increasingly intolerant of a biblical view of sexuality. The intolerance began during the so-called sexual revolution of the 1960s, and has been escalating ever since. Our culture has detached sexual relations from marriage, and consequently has gone from acceptance of various sexual experiences to celebration of them. Increasingly, people who believe that sex is designed for heterosexual relations within a marriage bond are ridiculed, despised, criminalized, and marginalized. In 2015 a major event raised the opposition to the biblical viewpoint a couple notches higher. Specifically, in June of that year the Supreme Court handed down a decision supporting same-sex marriage. The consequence has been a rapidly increasing adversarial relationship between America's secular culture and biblical Christianity on the topic of sexuality. More than ever before, this topic is at the forefront of Americans' minds almost constantly.

Creation matters because it addresses sexual relations unblinkingly. This brief study is not intended to deal with the breadth and depth of these things, but rather to show how the Christian belief in creation informs and guides our thinking about them.

We tend to think of sexuality in physiological, psychological, and moral terms. These are important categories as we seek to understand our sexuality. Yet, these are not the only categories needed to guide our thinking. In fact, if we limit ourselves to only those three categories, we cannot develop a truly biblical view of sexuality. We must introduce a fourth category into the mix, and in fact this is the most important one of the four because it is foundational to the other three. Specifically, we need to think about our sexuality in terms of creation.

When God made human beings in His image, He made them male and female, to be joined in a complementary relationship of marriage. Therefore, the Bible objects to homosexuality primarily because of creation. More than violating a moral law, homosexuality subverts the image of God which is reflected in the two sexes – *a man shall leave his father and mother and be joined to his wife, and the two shall become one flesh*, Matthew 19:5. The Bible understands the lure of all kinds of sexual activity outside of heterosexual marriage, and it forbids those things based on how God created us, not based on arbitrary and antiquated standards imposed on us by a legalistic deity who wants to suppress our legitimate deep longings. Simply put: Heterosexuality within a marriage relationship is part of original creation, and moral laws that forbid fornication, adultery, and homosexuality are derived from that original design.

We should note two things about the Matthew 19:4-6 passage. First, Jesus Himself affirmed Moses' account of creation: "Have you not read?" He did not refer to it as symbolic or fanciful, but rather as a historical fact which served as the basis for His teaching about marriage and divorce. Second, He affirmed the biblical model for heterosexuality. It was male-and-female from the very start, and still is so. Our complementary maleness and our femaleness are part of original creation and are reflective of the one true God. If we believe that Jesus' word is authoritative, then we are obliged to affirm what He said about our sexuality

RESPOND TO IT

1. Discuss: "[T]he Bible objects to homosexuality primarily because of creation. More than violating a moral law, homosexuality subverts the image of God which is reflected in the two sexes."

2. In what ways do our maleness and our femaleness reflect the image of God?

3. Does accepting this view of sexuality mean that people will never struggle with non- traditional sexual impulses?

38
ANTHROPOLOGY
NOT ANIMALS

Creation matters because humans are not animals.

Genesis 1:28

God blessed them; and God said to them, "Be fruitful and multiply, and fill the earth, and subdue it; and rule over the fish of the sea and over the birds of the sky and over every living thing that moves on the earth."

Genesis 2:20

The man gave names to all the cattle, and to the birds of the sky, and to every beast of the field, but for Adam there was not found a helper suitable for him.

Psalm 8:6-8

6You make him to rule over the works of Your hands;
You have put all things under his feet,
7All sheep and oxen,
And also the beasts of the field,
8The birds of the heavens and the fish of the sea,
Whatever passes through the paths of the seas.

There have been two pervasive ideas about humans and animals afloat for a long time. One is that the mandate in Genesis 1:28 is a God-given excuse to abuse animals. That idea has been proven wrong repeatedly, yet secularists continue to accuse Bible-believers of it. It is wrong for three reasons. The first is that God gave the command prior to Adam's sin, so there was no such thing as abuse at that time. The second is that while the word "rule" means to "have dominion over," it does not mean to do so oppressively. "Ruling" can be righteous and kind, or brutal, and we need to look at other words in the context to determine which kind of ruling is in view. In this context, it is the righteous kind of ruling. Third, if there have been people who have used this verse as a justification to be harsh to animals, their misinterpretation and perverted application do not prove that the verse is a mandate to abuse animals. On the contrary, it proves that there is a correct interpretation that should be followed in practice. Wrong interpretations of Scripture do not prove that Scripture is wrong, but that the interpreters are wrong.

A second pervasive idea is that since humans share many of the physical characteristics of mammals, there is nothing that sets us apart from mammals, and we are animals just as they are. This has a humorous side when someone says, "Animals are people, too." Of course, no one whose mind is not unhinged actually believes that. On the more serious side are the animal rights activists who are becoming more extreme in their assertions of the biological and moral equivalence of humans and animals.

These people will probably not be persuaded by a Christian's responses. The reason is that we derive our perspective on the distinction between animals and humans from the Bible, particularly from its teaching about creation. Secularists scoff at such reasoning. At this point we need to decide if we really believe the Bible. If the Bible is actually true in its teaching that humans are not animals, then we need to confidently and gently point out some things to the people who oppose this idea.

There are still non-Christians who do not yet see humans and animals as equivalent, but their numbers are diminishing. They inherently know that there is something distinctive about humans. Everyone ought to be able to see that humans do things that animals do not do – We build cities, discuss ideas, create organizations, conduct scientific experiments, set up charities, pray, read and write, create works of art, invent things, use language to communicate, and do many other uniquely human things. Additionally, we have an inner sense of worth that animals just do not seem to possess, apart from their God-given drive for self-preservation and protection of their young. We project our own feelings onto our pets, and assume that they feel the same way. Thanks to many Disney cartoons, we have been led to think that animals have the same emotions and self-consciousness that humans have. That idea belongs right where it originated, in cartoons.

Beginning in Genesis, original creation contained animals and humans, separate and distinct, although similar in many ways. They share some common designs because they have a common Designer. God told the first humans to "rule over" the animal kingdom, not to live alongside it as equals. Their rule was to be wise, benevolent, and strong, but never foolish and abusive.

Among all the animals, some of which had physical similarities to Adam, there were none that would be a right mate for him. There were no near-human women who could be a wife. There was a wall of separation between Adam and all animals. Only another human would be suitable for him. That is still true. This truth should help our current generation draw in the reins somewhat on our obsession with our pets. They are gifts of God to us, but after all is said and done, they are animals, quite unlike humans who are made in the image of God.

With regard to the humans-animals question, we are separate and unequal.

RESPOND TO IT

1. Discuss: Humans are unlike animals in that we were created specially by God in His image. That cannot be said of any animal.

2. Agree/Disagree: With regard to the humans-animals question, we are separate and unequal.

3. How does this study affect your view of pets?

39
ANTHROPOLOGY
DIGNITY

Creation matters because it is the reason why racism is a sin and why we all have worth.

Genesis 1:26-27

26Then God said, "Let Us make man in Our image, according to Our likeness; and let them rule over the fish of the sea and over the birds of the sky and over the cattle and over all the earth, and over every creeping thing that creeps on the earth." 27God created man in His own image, in the image of God He created him; male and female He created them.

Genesis 5:1

This is the book of the generations of Adam. In the day when God created man, He made him in the likeness of God.

Genesis 9:6

"Whoever sheds man's blood, By man his blood shall be shed, For in the image of God He made man.

Psalm 86:9

All nations whom You have made shall come and worship before You, O LORD,
And they shall glorify Your name.

Psalm 100:3

Know that the LORD Himself is God;
It is He who has made us, and not we ourselves;
We are His people and the sheep of His pasture.

All humans have dignity because all humans are made in the image of God. Creation is the answer to racial and ethnic conflict. It is the answer to our overinflated and underinflated senses of worth.

Several years ago I was in a meeting where the speaker asked the audience, "How many races are there on earth?" Most people, by a show of hands, answered at least four. The correct answer was one — the human race. The speaker's reasons were both *theological* — all humans have the same Creator and are made in the image of God — and *scientific* — all humans' genetic profiles are nearly identical, espcially when compared to those of animals. The genetic causes for differences in skin color, eye color, hair, etc. are relatively minor, and in no way do they affect our mutual humanness. All so-called races share a common human genetic make-up and a common Creator. Therefore, racism based on physical differences is a reflection of sin in human hearts derived from a lack of knowing the Creator and who we actually are.

Racism is a cultural and relational sin, and it is more than that — it is a sin against the Creator. The Bible barely notes "race" as we define it today, and it stands firmly against anyone who hates, oppresses, despises, or harms another person due to so-called racial differences.

Our modern world has made racism a complex, knotty, social-political problem. By contrast, the Bible neither treats it dismissively nor overcomplicates it. The Scriptures give us more than a moral code that says, "Don't be racists." Rather they tell us who we are and where we came from, namely that every human being is an image bearer of God, and every human being can trace our ancestry back to our original parents, Adam and Eve. Psalm 89:6 talks about "all nations whom You have made." We cannot look anywhere on earth and find people who were not made by God. Therefore, there is absolutely no rationale for racism in Christianity. Christianity is anti-racism, regardless of how some people over the years have misused the Scriptures to justify it.

Because God made us all in His image, we all have worth and dignity. As image bearers we are set above all other life-forms. Our lives have value primarily for this reason. There is no human life that does not have value and dignity. It should be unthinkable for us to look at a person who is made in the image of God and say that he or she has no worth, or even less worth than ourselves or someone else.

Moving in another direction, this is also the starting place for dealing with personal feelings of inadequacy and worthlessness. This is not a simplistic theology-pill that will instantly solve these feelings, but it is an essential foundation. This goes to the core of who we are, not just to our physical and psychological make-up or the incidentals of our lives.

As we become convinced of our worth and dignity, the Bible simultaneously teaches us about humility. Interestingly, the rationale for humility is the same as for our dignity, namely that we are created. We had absolutely nothing to do with our existence. We are made, so we should be humble. We are made in God's image, so we have dignity. Those two truths are like railroad tracks. We need to run on both of the rails.

The doctrine of creation should shape our thinking about two things: Race and Self-worth. We all know that secularists have their own reasons to deplore racism and to affirm self-worth, and they have some wise, helpful insights. The only problem is that their solutions are built on the shifting sands of human wisdom, sociology, and psychology. Because of creation, racism is forbidden. And, because of creation, every human being has dignity and worth. Creation is the firm foundation upon which these two truths rest unchangingly.

RESPOND TO IT

1. How would you explain your views on racism to another Christian? To a non-Christian?

2. Discuss why we need to run on the twin rails of humility and dignity.

3. How would you use the doctrine of creation to help someone who is struggling with self-worth?

4. How does creation address the problem of racism?

40
ANTHROPOLOGY
Respect

Creation matters because it tell
us how we should respond to God.

Revelation 14:7

and he said with a loud voice, "Fear God, and give Him glory, because the hour of His judgment has come; worship Him who made the heaven and the earth and sea and springs of waters."

Ecclesiastes 12:1

Remember also your Creator in the days of your youth, before the evil days come and the years draw near when you will say, "I have no delight in them."

Isaiah 29:16

You turn things around!
Shall the potter be considered as equal with the clay,
That what is made would say to its maker, "He did not make me";
Or what is formed say to him who formed it, "He has no understanding"?

Isaiah 45:9

"Woe to the one who quarrels with his Maker—
An earthenware vessel among the vessels of earth!

Will the clay say to the potter, 'What are you doing?'
Or the thing you are making say, 'He has no hands'?

Perhaps this study could be included with the earlier ones that focused on who the Creator God is, but since the verses here look at the human response to the Creator, it seems best to include it in the Anthropology group of studies.

By now it should be clear that creation is not a ho-hum topic. It is the first thing that the Bible tells us about God, and it pervades the entirety of Scripture. When the thought of creation really grabs hold of our minds and hearts, it should evoke at least three respect-filled responses toward the Creator.

1ST RESPONSE -- WORSHIP

The idea of worship as our first response to the Creator God is a recurring theme in the Bible, as I have already shown in these studies. Romans 1:20-21 builds on this theme and tells us the wrong way to respond to creation: *20 For since the creation of the world His invisible attributes, His eternal power and divine nature, have been clearly seen, being understood through what has been made, so that they are without excuse. 21 For even though they knew God, they did not honor Him as God or give thanks.* Turning these verses around, we see the right way to respond – honor the Creator and give thanks, in a word, worship. That is the right way to respond when we observe the beauty, enormity, intricacy, and complexity of creation, all of which point to an even greater Creator.

We know that we should worship and praise God, but we often have a hard time figuring out exactly what worship is, and we are not always sure how to link our minds and hearts to it. Looking at worship in purely human terms, it is something that gets us outside ourselves. When we worship someone, we are absorbed with his or her beauty, accomplishments, and/or abilities, and we are barely self-conscious as we worship. Worship is a choice, not a feeling. It is an action, not an experience. It has little to do with our feelings, and everything to do with the person we are worshiping. It can be quiet or exuberant. It can be private or with others.

Praise is one expression of our worship. We praise God for various things like His faithfulness, His love, His power, His omniscience, and His protection. And that is all good. If nothing comes to mind, some people simply pray, "Lord, I praise You for who You are." When I hear that last one I sometimes wonder, "Is that the best you can come up with?" But first and foremost, God wants us to worship Him because He is the Creator.

In the future, at the climax of human history, the hosts of heaven will draw our attention to one specific truth about God, namely that He is the Creator of everything, Revelation 14:7. Even in the tumultuous final days of earth history, God will want us to be firmly grounded in the doctrine of creation. And He will want us to go beyond simply knowing that He is the Creator to remaining faithful and worshiping Him for that reason. That knowledge and that response will sustain Christians during those final days, and by implication, during the centuries prior to them. Creation is not just a piece of information, it is the number one reason to worship God.

2ND RESPONSE -- REMEMBER

When the Bible says "remember," it is saying something more than when a school teacher tells students to remember certain information that will show up later on a test. It is like when a parent tells a child who is going out the door, "Remember what I told you about not talking to strangers." Also, it is like the old battle cry, "Remember the Alamo!" In the former example, remembering ought to cause obedience, inspiration, and motivation.

Ecclesiastes 12:1 wraps obedience, inspiration, and motivation together in its exhortation. It is noteworthy that the verse does not say, "Remember your powerful God" or "Remember your Savior," but "Remember your Creator." This remembering is an activity that should begin when we are young and continue throughout our lives. We should not think of it as something that we can put off until things get difficult. It is a habit that will navigate us through the ups-and-downs of our lives. If we start doing it at a young age, we will be prepared for the future troubles that will inevitably come, and by remembering our Creator we will be more likely to be motivated to remain faithful to Him, to handle things obediently, and to know that we are in the safe hands of Him who made and oversees everything.

3RD RESPONSE – STOP ARGUING

Sooner or later, maybe often, we won't like the way things are going in our lives, or we might object to the way we are made. If we are honest, we might admit that we wish God would do things a little more to our liking. So we gripe against Him. We are pretty sure we should not do that, but we just can't help ourselves. We complain that He doesn't step in and fix things. Actually, God does not hold it against us if we bring our complaints to Him. He would rather we do that than to turn away from Him and grumble or curse to ourselves or to others. The psalms are filled with complaints, and they actually teach us how to do it. But God does not want us to get stuck in our complaints, and He gives us an exit out of them, and it is this: remember that He is our Creator and know that He is working out His will. The two verses from Isaiah above warn us against taking our complaints to the next level, namely presuming that we have a right to tell God where He has gone wrong, what He should do and how He should do it. When we start to do that, we are overstepping our bounds. It shows that we are ignoring the fact that He is our Maker. As our Maker, He knows everything about us, what is best for us, and how we should get on in this world. He has things under control, even if we cannot see it or like it. We may be weighed down by our circumstances, but remembering that God is our Maker, we should be able to trust that He is lovingly caring for us, even when it does not feel like it.

RESPOND TO IT

1. Give some non-religious examples of worship.

2. Discuss: If we do not worship God, we will worship something else, either ourselves or some other created thing, thereby dehumanizing ourselves.

3. How can we complain to God without sinning? Realistically, how can we move from complaining to God to peacefully trusting Him?

4. How has remembering something inspired you, motivated you, and/or caused you to be obedient.

COSMOLOGY

Cosmology is the study of the origin, development, and nature of the universe. When we look up we see all kinds of things, such as clouds, blue sky, sun, moon, stars, planets, and comets. Where did these things come from? What laws of science govern them? The Bible addresses these questions in the doctrine of creation, and that is what studies 41-45 explore.

41
COSMOLOGY
ASSUMING

Creation matters because it provides basic explanations about the origin of everything.

There are many competing explanations for the origin of everything. In the United States these can be boiled down to two most common ones –

1) a naturalistic one, represented by various Big Bang theories

2) a supernaturalistic one, represented by various creationist theories

According to the first, there has always been something physical. That "something" was small and contained a huge amount of energy. One day billions of years ago, for some unknown reason, it suddenly exploded – a.k.a. "Big Bang" – and formed the entire known universe quickly. After that everything developed naturally.

According to the second, there has always been the triune God, but nothing else. Then at some point in the past, for some reason known only to Him, He made the entire known universe out of nothing. From that initial point, He created, formed, and fashioned everything in the universe.

In some superficial ways, the two models resemble each other, but fundamentally they have significant differences. Some of those are the following:

1) The Big Bang began with something physical, but Creation began with nothing physical.

2) The Big Bang was an unguided explosion, but Creation was 100% guided.

3) The Big Bang was impersonal, but Creation was personal.

4) The Big Bang was purposeless, but Creation was purposeful.

5) The Big Bang has no explanation for what caused it to happen, but Creation has a definite explanation.

6) The Big Bang was caused exclusively by physical forces, but Creation was caused exclusively by words spoken by God.

There are more differences, but these are sufficient to show that the Big Bang and Creation are two entirely different interpretations of the origin of the universe rather than two versions of the same interpretation.

Here we will not look at a scientific comparison of the two models. Rather, we will look at a few biblical assertions that support Creation, beginning with the most basic one, namely that God made the heavens and the earth. He made every galaxy, star, moon, planet, comet, and asteroid, as well as everything on earth.

Nehemiah 9:6
"You alone are the LORD.
You have made the heavens,
The heaven of heavens with all their host,
The earth and all that is on it,
The seas and all that is in them.
You give life to all of them
And the heavenly host bows down before You.

Psalm 102:25
"Of old You founded the earth,
And the heavens are the work of Your hands.

Psalm 115:15

May you be blessed of the LORD,
Maker of heaven and earth.

These affirmations are repeated often in the Scriptures. The point is, there is nothing on earth or in the heavens that He did not make. This is a shared belief of both the Old and New Testaments.

Genesis 1 is foundational to creationists' beliefs, although there are different ways to interpret the passage. For example, the sequence of Genesis 1 is troubling for many Christians because it tells us in verses 14-19 that the sun, moon, and stars were created on the fourth day. That is after the earth was created, after there was already light, after there were already evenings and mornings, after there was vegetation, and after there were waters above and on the earth.

Some people try to address the issue by denying that the days in Genesis 1 are sequential. These people interpret them as thematic rather than as periods of time. The difficulties with that interpretation are: (1) It is inconsistent with every other literal and symbolic use of the word "day" in the Old Testament, where it always refers to time, not to literary themes. (2) It does not give due credence to the repeated phrase "evening and morning," the intent of which is to indicate the passage of time, rather than the transition from one theme to another. (3) It claims to see something, namely a thematic paradigm for Genesis 1, that all the writers of Scripture missed. Nowhere in the rest of the Bible is this thematic interpretation presented. So this interpretation has some appeal, but I think there is a better way to understand the sequence in Genesis 1. It helps if we look at two unnecessary assumptions that cause people to be troubled.

Looking at this sequence-of-days issue from a purely scientific perspective, it is troubling only if you make two unnecessary assumptions:

First unnecessary assumption:
The earth was created simultaneously with all other heavenly bodies.

In response to the first unnecessary assumption, people who espouse it are either:

(a) unable to conceptually imagine realities outside the observable physical world, and/or

(b) they are not theologically grounded, and/or

(c) they are not practical.

Regarding (a) — Looking at this conceptually, or perhaps I can say imaginatively, God has given human beings remarkable imaginations which we have used throughout our history to make incredible advances in everything we explore and do. We imagine artificial intelligence, driverless cars, a Big Bang, and cures for cancer. So why do we shut off our imaginations when it comes to the creation week? In other words, why do we think of the creation of the earth only in terms of processes that we currently observe? Why assume that the earth was necessarily created simultaneously with everything else?

We need to be careful to avoid being inconsistent in our faith. On one hand a Christian would say, "Oh, I can imagine Christ rose from the dead because God is powerful and could accomplish such a thing, and besides that, the Bible says it happened." But then, on the other hand, that same Christian might also say, "Oh, I can't imagine that the sequence of the creation events described in Genesis 1 actually happened that way." Yet the same two foundational underpinnings would still apply: God is powerful and could do it, and the Bible says it happened that way. If creation was a unique series of events in the history of the universe, the period of time when it was being constructed, why should we have trouble imagining that God did some things in unusual, unrepeated ways?

Regarding (b) -- Looking at this theologically, if God indeed created everything and is supremely powerful and wise, wouldn't He be capable of creating things in the sequence noted in Genesis 1 while sustaining His creation through each successive period of time? He is not bound to the laws of nature that operate in our current world, laws that He Himself created.

Regarding (c) -- Looking at the creation of the heavens and earth practically, we can picture it as the original and most magnificent construction project in history. Looking at creation like this, we find a helpful analogy in the techniques that contractors use to enable the construction of a house to move forward. I have already alluded to this above. For example, before the roof is installed they may cover the framework with tarps. Prior to the installation of various utilities, they usually run in electricity through generators, provide portable restrooms, and bring in bottled water. All of these temporary things are removed when the permanent alternatives are put into place. Similarly, God could easily have temporarily propped up and supported His developing creation throughout the whole process, and removed whatever props He may have used when creation was complete. We just need to remember that life is not "normal" during the construction process. Creation was an incredible construction project, and we would be misguided to insist that God was restricted by all the current laws of nature, geology, and astronomy during that process.

Second unnecessary assumption:
Vegetation, light, and evening-and-morning cycles cannot exist without heavenly bodies, especially the sun.

In response to this second unnecessary assumption, why must light on earth always have had the sun as its source? Couldn't God have lighted the earth on days one through three in some other way? Why would vegetation be impossible without the sun, particularly if God had provided some other source of light? Perhaps the original light had the same source that the future everlasting light will have, namely God Himself—

Revelation 22:5

And there will no longer be any night; and they will not have need of the light of a lamp nor the light of the sun, because the Lord God will illumine them; and they will reign forever and ever.

The point is, the creation process was a unique, unrepeatable event in history. It was a supernatural time. Things were different during that time from any time since then. It is illogical to try to superimpose upon the creation process our ideas about how it must have happened based on the way things operate now. During the creation period, God was building, propping up, and sustaining each phase of His creation as He proceeded to each successive phase.

Admittedly, the rest of Scripture does not make a big deal explicitly of the earth being created prior to the sun, moon, and stars. But that does not mean we can disregard or dismiss it. Genesis 1 gives us a very specific, locked-in sequence of creation, and whether we read that chapter as literal prose, "elevated prose," poetry, or some other ancient literary style, we cannot escape the text's assertion that the heavenly bodies came into existence after the creation of the earth.

If we believe that the Bible is the inspired Word of God, we should be unwilling to change it to accommodate current ideas. We may need to dig deep and do serious study on matters like this, but we must do so without manipulating the text of Scripture. Every Christian needs to pre-decide whether or not he or she actually believes that the Bible is the Word of God, and whether or not he or she is willing to hold to it even if current philosophies, scientific theories, and cultural practices seem to contradict it. We also need to interpret the Scriptures rightly, realizing that doing so requires far more than cursory readings and superficial conclusions.

In summary:

- Nowhere does the Bible express embarrassment or doubt about the sequence of the creation week.

- Everywhere the Bible affirms that God is the "Maker" of the heavens and the earth.

- Everywhere the Bible affirms God's sovereign power and control over His creation.

By His power He could have made everything in the exact order recorded in Genesis 1, and He could have sustained everything on each successive day until it all was complete.

This leads to an important conclusion. If we trust the Bible's description of how the world began, we will have a greater ability to trust its description of who we are and how the world should operate.

RESPOND TO IT

1. Do you agree that the two "assumptions" noted above are truly "unnecessary?" Do you agree with the responses to those assumptions?

2. Discuss the final sentence in this study: "If we trust the Bible's description of how the world began, we will have a greater ability to trust its description of who we are and how the world should operate."

3. Agree/Disagree: We Christians are too ready to accommodate our biblical beliefs to prevailing scientific ideas.

42
COSMOLOGY
STRETCHED OUT

*Creation matters because it gives insight
into the structure of the cosmos.*

Isaiah 40:22

*It is He who sits above the circle of the earth,
And its inhabitants are like grasshoppers,
Who stretches out the heavens like a curtain
And spreads them out like a tent to dwell in.*

Isaiah 42:5

*Thus says God the LORD,
Who created the heavens and stretched them out,
Who spread out the earth and its offspring,
Who gives breath to the people on it
And spirit to those who walk in it,*

Isaiah 44:24

*Thus says the LORD, your Redeemer, and the one who formed you
from the womb,
"I, the LORD, am the maker of all things,
Stretching out the heavens by Myself
And spreading out the earth all alone,*

Isaiah 51:13

That you have forgotten the LORD your Maker,
Who stretched out the heavens
And laid the foundations of the earth...

Jeremiah 10:12

It is He who made the earth by His power,
Who established the world by His wisdom;
And by His understanding He has stretched out the heavens.

Zechariah 12:1

The burden of the word of the LORD concerning Israel.
Thus declares the LORD who stretches out the heavens, lays the
foundation of the earth, and forms the spirit of man within him,

God's technique in making the heavens was to "stretch" them out. This is where some people see similarities between creation and the Big Bang, and at a basic level that is a valid observation. In both cases we see a vast expanded, and expanding, universe. In both cases heavenly bodies are stretched out in all directions. In both cases there is a probable point of origin from which all is stretched out.

The biblical teaching about the stretching out of the heavens is consistent with our astronomical observations. This fact is probably meaningless to secularists, but it should be reassuring to believers. These biblical assertions about the creation of the heavens lead to a few corollaries:

FIRST – TIME.

God created time as well as everything else. In stretching out the heavens, God inserted motion into His creation. Motion cannot exist apart from time; it is always a function of time, such as miles-per-hour. Hence, we conclude the obvious, God created not only the three physical dimensions of length, width, and height, but also the fourth dimension of time. Apart from God Himself, nothing exists outside of time. Everything on earth or that we experience takes place in time.

Second – Outer boundaries.

Perhaps there is an outer edge to the universe. If the Big Bang is true, then there is necessarily a place beyond which nothing exists. If creation is true, then there may be more out there than the Big Bang would anticipate, but the Scriptures are silent on that subject, and neither do they teach that the universe is infinite. If it were, it would be equal to God in that respect, but no created thing, even the universe, is equal to Him. As vast, complex, and powerful as the universe is, it is finite. It is marvelous, beautiful, awe-inspiring, and possibly even frightening, but it is merely a physical creation, designed, made, and superintended by the triune God.

We can only make cautious deductions about the outer edges of the universe based on our observations and what Scripture does say. For example, if we could miraculously arrive at the most distant star ever discovered, what would we see? More stars and galaxies? Something else? Nothing? We do not know. Whatever it would be, we can confidently say that it is part of God's design and creation. One thing we do know is that we can never come to a place where God's creation ends and something else starts, as if God's creation were in the neighborhood of other deities' creations. Nor can we come to a place where God is not there.

Third – Still stretching.

Isaiah 40:22 says that God "stretches out the heavens" (present tense). That verse could be interpreted to mean either that God is still doing what He did in the beginning, or that the power of God is revealed in the expanding heavens. If we understand the verse as saying that God is still stretching out the heavens, this is consistent with our observations that the universe is expanding.

On the other hand, if we understand the verse to describe the power of God, it would be like Isaiah was saying: "This is the kind of God our Creator is, He is a heavens-stretching God." Sometimes the Bible uses present tense verbs in referring to past events in order to either state an unchanging truth or to put the reader vividly into a situation that occurred in the past. Since several other passages, including some from Isaiah, refer to the stretching out of the heavens as something that has occurred in the past, I lean toward the interpretation that the verse uses the present tense verb in order to describe a permanent truth about Him, rather than saying that He is continuing to stretch out the heavens. This view still recognizes that the universe is expanding, and that it is doing so consistently with the laws of astrophysics that God originally designed into it. Whichever interpretation is correct, there is a central truth in the verse: creation is the explanation for the expanded and expanding universe.

RESPOND TO IT

1. As we sit on earth and gaze into the sky, what does it matter that God stretched out the heavens?

2. What is the significance of Isaiah 44:24 saying that God stretched out the heavens "by Myself," and spread out the earth "all alone?"

3. What are some implications of the fact that time itself was created by God?

43
COSMOLOGY
STARRY, STARRY NIGHT

*Creation matters because it explains
the arrangement of the heavens.*

Isaiah 40:26
*Lift up your eyes on high
And see who has created these stars,
The One who leads forth their host by number,
He calls them all by name;
Because of the greatness of His might and the strength of His power,
Not one of them is missing.*

Amos 5:8
*He who made the Pleiades and Orion
And changes deep darkness into morning,
Who also darkens day into night,
Who calls for the waters of the sea
And pours them out on the surface of the earth,
The LORD is His name.*

Job 9:8-9
*8Who alone stretches out the heavens
And tramples down the waves of the sea;
9Who makes the Bear, Orion and the Pleiades,
And the chambers of the south;*

Psalm 147:4

He counts the number of the stars;
He gives names to all of them.

WE CAN LOOK AT THE SKY THROUGH SEVERAL LENSES:

- The Romance lens. Through it we see the beauty of the heavens, but are unconcerned about scientific explanations. This is the lovers' lens and it evokes feelings of awe and romance.

- The So-What lens. Through it we observe all that we can see out there, and say to ourselves, "It just is what it is." This lens appeals to rationalists who are basically unaffected by what they see through it, apart from the information it provides.

- The Astrology lens. Through this lens mystics think they see heavenly influences that control our lives.

- The gods lens. This lens is like the Astrology one, but through it people see the heavens as created by, populated by, and/or owned by a host of gods who may or may not care about human life.

- The Astronomy lens. This is the explorers' lens, and through it they thrill at the possibility of discovering more and more heavenly bodies. For the secular scientist, this lens comes with a Big Bang filter.

- The Deist lens. This lens appeals to those who believe that there may have been a god who made everything, but who then retreated into an unseen heavenly dwelling, and is allowing it to run according to the laws of science that he built into it.

- The Biblical lens. Through it we see the heavens as they really are, created by the one true God.

The Biblical lens has some things in common with a couple of the other lenses. For example, like the Astronomy lens, it shows us the heavens as they actually are, but without the Big Bang filter. Like the Deist lens, it shows us a universe made by a supreme being, but not an aloof one. Like the Romance lens, it shows us the inspiring beauty of creation, but without the consequent glorification of the creation itself. Unlike the other lenses, the Biblical lens comes with an owner's manual. It discloses that there is a Creator God who designed what we see and that He has revealed Himself to us. It instructs us that we are not the product of purely naturalistic processes. If we look through the Astronomy lens, we see only physical heavenly bodies that operate by the laws of nature, some of which are mysterious or even unknown to us. Through that lens we see a random, vast array of stars and galaxies that are in their places as the result of a huge explosion. Actually, they are not so much in locations as on trajectories away from their point of origin. Since they are so far away, we can see only where they were eons ago. That raises the curious possibility that some or all of them no longer exist. Through the Astronomy lens we see only history, not present reality, due to the length of time that is required for light from them to reach the earth.

Through the Biblical lens we see expansion, movement in the heavens above. We should expect that based on the verses that describe God as stretching out the heavens. He did not simply suspend all the heavenly bodies motionless in space, but rather put each on its celestial path, a trajectory on which it travels.

Without an owner's manual we would see only the random arrangement of heavenly bodies that the Astronomy lens reveals. But the manual tells us that the arrangement is by design. At least twice we are told that the stars and constellations in the northern and southern hemispheres are the work of God's hand (Job 9:8-9 and Amos 5:8). We are not told why the heavens are arranged as they are, but we are told that they are definitely arranged and who did it.

This leads us to the next thing that we see, namely a vast number of stars. We are not even able to count them all, but God did. Not only that, but He named them all (Psalm 147:4). When we look into the sky, we see things that were designed, made, named, and arranged by the Lord God. The heavens reveal God's astronomical power and intelligence. They also reveal His personhood because only persons are able to name things.

When astronomers return to their telescopes night after night, they occasionally make new discoveries, but none have yet said something like, "Hey! Where did the Big Dipper go?! I know it was there yesterday, but now I can't find it!" This may be what Isaiah was getting at when he said about the stars, "Not one of them is missing." He knew that God is in control of every celestial body. Even the wandering planets, asteroids, and comets don't go missing; they just follow the paths God established for them. A star that collapses and then explodes is not "missing," but rather it is doing precisely what God wants it to do, when He wants it to happen, and how He directs it to happen. It is revealing God's power and wisdom.

RESPOND TO IT

1. Fill in the blank: When I look at the heavens, I see

   _____ .

2. On a scale of 1-5, where 1 means it does not matter at all and 5 means it matters significantly, rate how much it matters that the earth is placed where it is in the vast universe. Discuss your answer.

3. What does it matter to us to know that God has named all the stars?

44
COSMOLOGY
ANNOUNCING

Creation matters because it reveals
important things about the one true God.

Psalm 19:1-2

1*The heavens are telling of the glory of God;*

And their expanse is declaring the work of His hands.

2*Day to day pours forth speech, And night to night reveals knowledge.*

Romans 1:18-23

18*For the wrath of God is revealed from heaven against all ungodliness and unrighteousness of men who suppress the truth in unrighteousness,* 19*because that which is known about God is evident within them; for God made it evident to them.* 20*For since the creation of the world His invisible attributes, His eternal power and divine nature, have been clearly seen, being understood through what has been made, so that they are without excuse.* 21*For even though they knew God, they did not honor Him as God or give thanks, but they became futile in their speculations, and their foolish heart was darkened.* 22*Professing to be wise, they became fools,* 23*and exchanged the glory of the incorruptible God for an image in the form of corruptible man and of birds and four-footed animals and crawling creatures.*

The stars are not just mere curiosities. They are signposts to the Creator God. And they are more than signposts, they are loudspeakers announcing to everyone that there is a God and that

He is glorious. If the heavens are amazing, how much more so is the One who made them?

There is a message written in the heavens above us. That message is like the Introduction chapter of a book. It is a message that all people can see and understand, although not all choose to believe it. For those who do believe it, the Bible is the remainder of the book. Psalm 19:1-2 elaborates on the message, telling us at least five things that every human being should be able to deduce by looking into the heavens:

1) We are not alone. There is a God.

2) He is a God of glory.

3) He is not just a force but is a personal God. The third person personal pronoun is used: "His hands."

4) He communicates a message through His creation. Communication words are used: "telling," "declaring," "speech," "reveals."

5) He works. Everything we see in the sky is "the work of His hands." Therefore, since He made all that, He is supremely powerful.

These five things alone, without any further information from the Bible, ought to lead first to an acknowledgement of God's existence and then to worship of Him.

The apostle Paul picked up these same themes in Romans 1:18-23. In those verses Paul launched into a description of the consequences of unbelief. In verses 16-17 he had already talked about the life and salvation that is given to those who believe the gospel. Starting in verse 18 he talked about those who do not believe. He described them as "suppressing the truth in unrighteousness," and the truth that they suppress is what they observe in creation. Rather than believing in and honoring the God who is revealed there, they worship creation itself, leading to futility, foolishness, sexual deviancy, depraved minds, and disintegrating relationships. At the root of societal and moral decay there is something of enormous significance – a failure to give glory to the Creator. This is why creation is essential to the apostle's teaching in Romans 1.

When Paul wanted people to understand who the one true God is, he did not back away from the truth of creation. Rather He appealed to it as the reason people should stand in awe of God and believe in Him. In Acts 14:15 he said, ...[*We*] *preach the gospel to you that you should turn from these vain things to a living God, who made the heaven and the earth and the sea and all that is in them.* Paul said those words to polytheists. By referring to creation he was underscoring the fact that there is one true God.

When Paul spoke to Greek philosophers in Athens, again he based his message on creation. In his address recorded in Acts 17:22-32, he said, *24 The God who made the world and all things in it, since He is Lord of heaven and earth... 25 He Himself gives to all people life and breath and all things; 26 and He made from one man every nation of mankind to live on all the face of the earth, having determined their appointed times and the boundaries of their habitation... 28 for in Him we live and move and exist... 31 He has fixed a day in which He will judge the world in righteousness through a Man whom He has appointed, having furnished proof to all men]by raising Him from the dead. 32 Now when they heard of the resurrection of the dead, some began to sneer...* In the face of likely opposition from secular intellectuals, he did not shrink from declaring the truth of creation. Their response should have been, and perhaps was, "Wow! That is an amazing God!" Interestingly, the passage in Acts 17 does not indicate that they objected to the idea of God as Creator. They seemed willing to go along with that. The thing that stopped the show was not creation but Paul's reference to the resurrection of Christ. Apparently these philosophers could believe that there is a God who is so powerful that He could create the heavens, the earth, and all human life, but they drew the line at the possibility that He could raise someone from the dead. For them, even the Creator God had His limits. In today's culture, the situation might be reversed, thanks to a plethora of "spiritualities" that are embraced by many Americans. If Paul were speaking at a secular university, the students might be willing to consider the idea of a resurrection, but they would laugh him off the podium if he seriously suggested that God had created the universe.

Consequently, presuppositions can blind us to something we all should see, namely that there is a God who created the heavens and the earth and who raises the dead, and we should stand in awe of Him. If and when we actually see that God both created and raises the dead, we should desire to know more about who that Creator is. This is where creation and the gospel meet.

The doctrine of creation is not just an academic, theological subject; it is a doxological subject. It should cause worship in addition to intellectual inquiry. In fact, worship should take priority.

RESPOND TO IT

1. "At the root of societal and moral decay there is something of enormous significance – a failure to give glory to the Creator." This is true of societies. Discuss how it also is true of individuals.

2. Romans 1:18 says: "For the wrath of God is revealed from heaven against all ungodliness and unrighteousness of men who suppress the truth in unrighteousness." Agree/Disagree: People reject the gospel not for intellectual reasons but because they do not want to give up their unrighteousness.

3. Do you agree that students at a secular university today might be more willing to accept the idea of resurrection from the dead than the idea of divine creation?

45
COSMOLOGY
ASTROPHYSICS

*Creation matters because it was when the
laws of astrophysics were established.*

Job 38:1, 31-33

1Then the LORD answered Job out of the whirlwind and said...

*31"Can you bind the chains of the Pleiades, Or loose the cords of
Orion? 32"Can you lead forth a constellation in its season, And guide
the Bear with her satellites? 33"Do you know the ordinances of the
heavens, Or fix their rule over the earth?*

Job had suffered greatly. His friends had come to comfort him,
but only added to his misery by accusing him of sin, which was
the only reason that they could imagine why God would do such
things to a person. Starting from that premise, they veered off into
other errors about the Lord and how He works. Overall Job had
responded rightly and wisely, but eventually even he was worn
down by a combination of his suffering and the accusations of his
friends, and he, too, began to go off the rails of truth about God
and himself.

In chapter 38 God interrupted the speeches, and He addressed
Job directly. When He finished, Job said in **Job 42:2-6:**
*2"I know that You can do all things,
And that no purpose of Yours can be thwarted.*

3'Who is this that hides counsel without knowledge?'
Therefore I have declared that which I did not understand,
Things too wonderful for me, which I did not know."
4'Hear, now, and I will speak; I will ask You, and You instruct me.'
5"I have heard of You by the hearing of the ear;
But now my eye sees You;
6Therefore I retract, And I repent in dust and ashes."

What did God say to Job that satisfied him and caused such a response? Did He explain the conversation with the devil in the court of heaven? No. Did He promise Job that everything would turn out alright in the end? No. Rather than offering reassuring words of comfort and explanation, God rebuked Job and his friends, and instructed Job about how He had designed the heavens, the earth, and all creatures on the earth. To our 21st century ears, God's message seems almost hard and insensitive, even unrelated to Job's suffering. Why would He talk about creation and His own power when this poor man has been struggling with great tragedies, grief, accusations, and illness? Why didn't God overwhelm Job with love, healing, comfort, and restoration? Why didn't God explain what was really behind the circumstances of Job's suffering? That is how we think God should have responded. But for Job, what God said was exactly what he needed to hear. Whether or not he would ever find relief from his suffering, Job was satisfied with the revelation he received from the Lord. God's revelation of Himself and His power over creation was sufficient to comfort Job.

The answer to Job's suffering was larger than his immediate circumstances and speculations about the justice of God. Job needed a framework within which to understand who God is – the Creator and sustainer of all things, animate and inanimate. Job needed to look beyond his immediate situation to the power, wisdom, and majesty of God.

In Job 38:31-33 the Lord directed Job's attention to laws of astrophysics – "the ordinances of the heavens" and "their rule over the earth." He told Job to look at several constellations, and asked him how much control he had over them or over the seasonal shifts in the stars. In that brief flash of understanding, Job knew that all the heavenly phenomena that he could observe were designed and completely controlled by God; nothing was accidental or random, but was directed by "ordinances" and "rules" that God had established. In other words, every physical law of astronomy, physics, and astrophysics was put into place by the Lord. He did more than create the stars, he set up the physical laws that govern them. If He could do that, He could do anything He pleased, including overseeing the circumstances of one man on earth. That lesson in astrophysics went deep into Job's soul. From it he was able to discern that the things that happened to him were within God's providential care. Even in Job's dreadful situation, and with no disclosure from the Lord regarding the devil's activities, and no assurance of restoration, he could rest in the knowledge that his life was in the hands of the majestic Creator. Job understood that the God who revealed Himself to him had left nothing to chance, in the heavens or on earth. He made everything and determined how everything should work, right down to the events in the lives of one man and his family.

That is what Job needed to hear, and he got the message. He was overwhelmed by the awesomeness of the Creator, not with any philosophical answers or gifts from God. He did not receive immediate relief after God's demonstration and lecture. His relief would come later, but he did not know that at the time. Nonetheless he was satisfied because now he knew the true sovereign Creator, and that was sufficient for him. For Job it was more important to know God than to know why bad things had happened to him. It led him to worship and bow in humble repentance before Him.

RESPOND TO IT

1. Incredibly, astrophysics was part of God's response to Job. Even more incredibly, Job was satisfied with that response. Why do you think God responded to Job in this way?

2. How can such truths from the book of Job bring comfort to us when we suffer?

3. How would God's speech to Job affect you if you were in Job's place?

GEOLOGY

Just as the earth is a subset of the universe, Geology is a subset of Cosmology. If we want to understand what kind of a world this is, we have two choices. One is to see everything as the result of purely random natural processes. In that scenario, nothing has any transcendent meaning, and we are entirely at the mercy of impersonal forces. A second scenario is to understand that the world is the creation of God. In this scenario, the earth and our lives on it have meaning, and are under His control.

Studies 46-50 examine several things that the Bible tells us about the earth on which we reside.

46
GEOLOGY
METEOROLOGY

*Creation matters because it is when God
established weather patterns.*

God not only created the earth, but He set up the "laws of nature" that govern it. In Job 38:33 God referred to ordinances He established that "rule over the earth." This would include not only astrophysics, but geology, geophysics, and meteorology. Much is said in the Scriptures about God's control of the climate, seasons, and weather. He not only controls these things, He is responsible for their existence.

Psalm 74:17
You have established all the boundaries of the earth;
You have made summer and winter.

Jeremiah 14:22
Are there any among the idols of the nations who give rain?
Or can the heavens grant showers?
Is it not You, O LORD our God?
Therefore we hope in You,
For You are the one who has done all these things.

Acts 14:17

and yet He did not leave Himself without witness, in that He did good and gave you rains from heaven and fruitful seasons, satisfying your hearts with food and gladness."

Job 38:26-30

26To bring rain on a land without people,

On a desert without a man in it,

27To satisfy the waste and desolate land

And to make the seeds of grass to sprout?

28"Has the rain a father?

Or who has begotten the drops of dew?

29"From whose womb has come the ice?

And the frost of heaven, who has given it birth?

30"Water becomes hard like stone,

And the surface of the deep is imprisoned.

An architect designs houses so people can prepare food, take care of personal hygiene, be safe, rest comfortably, and interact well. A good general contractor takes the architect's design and builds into the house many life-sustaining and comfort-producing features, such as electricity, plumbing, heating, cooling, and ventilation. Many other things go into the design and construction of a house, such as windows, proximity to other houses and markets, furnishings, building materials, and decorative features.

The point of the house illustration is fairly obvious. God, as both the Architect and the General Contractor of the earth, designed and built the world with such things in mind. Climate and weather are two of the vital systems that He included in our home planet.

A non-Christian would probably believe that meteorological phenomena are merely the result of natural forces at work over billions of years. Many people believe that massive weather patterns are human-caused. Despite the power, complexity, and order of these phenomena, those people see no reason to postulate a supernatural Creator. The Christian sees these phenomena through an entirely different lens. Obviously, we know that there are physical laws that govern seasons, climate, rain, and wind, but we see more. We see the wisdom and handiwork of a Master Designer.

Rain is one of the things that God designed and controls. Job 5:10 says, *He gives rain on the earth And sends water on the fields,* and Job 28:25 tells us, *When He set a limit for the rain And a course for the thunderbolt.* God, not Mother Nature, did that. In Acts 14:17 Paul and Barnabas declared rain to be one of the Lord's witnesses, *and yet He did not leave Himself without witness, in that He did good and gave you rains from heaven and fruitful seasons, satisfying your hearts with food and gladness.* According to the apostles, even non-Christians should have a hunch that there is a good Creator God behind every rainfall.

The Acts 14 passage adds another meteorological phenomenon to the witnesses of God: seasons. "He gave you...fruitful seasons." Most of us learned in our beginning science classes that the earth revolves around the sun once a year. Since the earth is slightly titled on its axis, the angle of the sunlight hitting the earth changes in the northern and southern hemispheres as the earth travels through space, and as a result we experience changing seasons. That is all so familiar to us that we barely give it any thought. The Bible might say to us, "Don't dismiss the changing seasons so quickly." In fact, the changing seasons are such a big deal that all people should observe them and realize that maybe, just maybe, there is a God who designed that.

Even in our scientific age we should be amazed at the intricate, complex combination of forces that cause seasons. The earth is just far enough away from the sun to prevent the seasons from being too hot or too cold. The rate at which the earth revolves around the sun is just right to prevent the seasons from being too short or too long. The rate at which the earth spins on its axis provides the necessary daily cycles of light and darkness for vegetation to thrive and for humans to work and rest. All of these things should awaken everyone to the reality of a good Creator.

Dew, ice, hail, clouds, wind, rain, storms, snow, cooling, warming are all attributed by the Scriptures to the Creator. He designed the world with such wisdom that all of these things contribute to life on this planet. Meteorology points to God the Creator.

RESPOND TO IT

1. To what extent do you really believe that God controls the weather?

2. How can you incorporate the biblical truths about meteorology into your prayers?

3. How is rain a "witness" to the Creator?

47

GEOLOGY

Land and Sea

*Creation matters because geologic stability
and scientific inquiry depend on it.*

Many people have a tendency to think that if we can explain something scientifically, God has nothing to do with it. We need to consider the possibility that perhaps we have things backward. Namely, perhaps we can explain things scientifically because God has everything to do with it. That is the foundational premise derived from Scripture that has been behind much of scientific inquiry over the centuries. Perhaps we have been made jittery by stories about people in the past who have attributed naturally-occurring phenomena, like solar eclipses, to miracles of God. The Bible does not call these things "miracles," but it is not skittish about attributing them to the Creator. It exhorts us to think more deeply about the Lord's working in the earth on which we reside. Not every natural event is a miracle, but every natural event is designed by God.

Assuming:

- God, acting alone, created everything, and
- God is rational, logical and unchanging,

we can conclude that:

- there is order, cause-and-effect, and inter-relationships in our physical world that we can observe and interpret.

Assuming:

- we are made in God's image with the ability to observe and reason, and

- God placed us in the created order,

we can conclude that:

- we are capable of rightly seeing and understanding what He has made.

Assuming:

- God created the earth and seas and all that is in them, and

- God established biological and geological boundaries,

we can conclude that:

- things are not in a state of flux. Elephants do not become poodles, humans do not become flamingos, mountains do not become marshmallows, and the earth and seas remain separated.

Job 38:8-11

8"Or who enclosed the sea with doors
When, bursting forth, it went out from the womb;
9When I made a cloud its garment
And thick darkness its swaddling band,
10And I placed boundaries on it
And set a bolt and doors,
11And I said, 'Thus far you shall come, but no farther;
And here shall your proud waves stop'?

Nehemiah 9:6

"You alone are the LORD.
You have made the heavens,
The heaven of heavens with all their host,
The earth and all that is on it,
The seas and all that is in them.
You give life to all of them
And the heavenly host bows down before You.

Psalm 104:9

You set a boundary that they may not pass over,
So that they will not return to cover the earth.

Jeremiah 5:22

'Do you not fear Me?' declares the LORD.
'Do you not tremble in My presence?
For I have placed the sand as a boundary for the sea,
An eternal decree, so it cannot cross over it.
Though the waves toss, yet they cannot prevail;
Though they roar, yet they cannot cross over it.

We stand in awe at the edge of an ocean as we see its beauty and vastness. We also tremble when we think about its power and fury, as when it sends hurricanes and tsunamis ashore. That is the same awe/fear response we should have as we contemplate the Lord and how He has designed everything. We should be amazed at the way He designed the incredible complexity and balance between earth and sea. We should marvel at His infinite creativity in making the amazing varieties of life that thrive on the earth and in the sea.

Besides awe and fear as we stand on the ocean's shore, we also should experience gratitude and peace. The reason is that we have assurance that the shoreline was drawn by God. The dry land on which we stand is secure. Occasional floods, earthquakes, and erosion notwithstanding, the earth and seas have been permanently put in their places by the power of the almighty Creator. A non-Christian may be awed by the ocean but merely thinks, "That is just how Mother Nature made it," and has no assurance that the dry earth will not suddenly be engulfed by the waters. The Christian has a very different perspective. We stand assured that the shoreline is fixed by the Lord and that He has decreed that it shall always remain so, based on Jeremiah 5:22.

Could there be a large earthquake that would cause parts of California's shoreline to slip into the ocean? Possibly, but we have not seen anything like that happening in recorded history, apart from erosion in various places and the calving of some glaciers in Alaska, both of which are minuscule by comparison, and hardly a negation of the assurances in the verses quoted above. There may be catastrophes like that sometime in the future, but they would not be a refutation of the verses quoted above. In fact, if and when such things happen, possibly they will be within the context of far larger events, namely the final days of planet earth.

A person might legitimately ask, "What about the flood of Noah's time? The seas definitely crossed their boundaries then." Actually, in that flood, more was happening than the seas rising past their boundaries. Something unique in the history of earth occurred. First, we need to remember that the flood was not just a natural catastrophe; it was the outpouring of God's judgment on the earth because of the constant evil that people were committing. Second, we need to remember that the flood was caused by a combination of unique events, namely that *on the same day all the fountains of the great deep burst open, and the floodgates of the sky were opened,* Genesis 7:11. We can speculate about what the "fountains" were, although we can be sure that they were not mere decorative fountains like we find in public squares. They were powerful enough to contribute to flooding the entire earth, and they did not merely start spraying water, but rather they "burst open."

Regarding the "floodgates of the sky," we can safely assume that this refers to physical forces that had previously held back torrential rains. When they were opened, they released something far more powerful and destructive than a gentle spring rain; they released a powerful storm unlike anything that has occurred on earth before or since. Third, we need to remember that when the flooding was finished, the waters receded, and once again there was dry earth and the seas. In today's terminology, Noah's flood was a "one off" event which God Himself promised never to repeat – "... *neither shall there again be a flood to destroy the earth,*" Genesis 9:11.

In Psalm 104:6 we read that there was a time when waters stood "above the mountains." Then in verse 8 we are told that "the mountains rose" and that "the valleys sank down," each to the places where they still are. That probably happened after the flood, because verse 7 says that the waters receded at God's "rebuke" and at the sound of His "thunder." Since original creation was all good and did not need rebuking, this event must have happened after sin entered the world. Also, there is no mention of thunder in Genesis 1, but elsewhere in Scripture we read of thunder accompanying God's judgment, such as during the flood.

Just as God separated the seas from the dry land in the original creation, so He did again after the flood. According to Job 38:10 and Jeremiah 5:22, God locked and bolted the waters so they will never again "cross over" the coastline. Psalm 104:9 reiterates this assurance. Likewise, in God's tutorial to Job on the creation of everything, He included His promise that the seas would permanently stop at coastlines. The same creative power that made the earth also established the post-flood land masses, with their fixed shorelines, and bodies of water.

At original creation God was not just in the business of drawing boundaries; He was also making all life on earth and in the seas. Regardless of how long we think it took, we should agree that God did that. When we study oceanology, biology and all the other life-sciences, we are studying more than things that appeared randomly through natural processes; we are studying things that God made.

The earth and the seas are not God, despite claims by some mystics. Also, God is not the earth and the seas, despite claims by pantheists. But neither is there a wall of separation between God and the world. He created it, He owns it, and He is still involved in it. We cannot find anything on this planet that is alien to God. There is no place on earth where we can get away from God. We cannot find anything that functions in isolation from Him. The boundaries of the earth and sea are stable, as are the laws of nature that govern this planet and life on it.

RESPOND TO IT

1. Agree/Disagree: Typically we think that if we can explain something scientifically, God has nothing to do with it.

2. The next time you stand at the edge of the ocean, what are some things that you might think about in light of the verses quoted above?

3. Discuss whether are not the verses quoted in this study are promises that sections of the California coast will never be plunged into the ocean due to a catastrophic earthquake.

48
GEOLOGY
LIKE A ROCK

Creation matters because it is why the
earth is stable until the end.

Psalm 119:89-91

89Forever, O LORD,
Your word is settled in heaven.
90Your faithfulness continues throughout all generations;
You established the earth, and it stands.
91They stand this day according to Your ordinances,
For all things are Your servants.

Look around and what do you see? Earthquakes, changing landscapes, sinkholes, erosion, melting glaciers, and so forth. Now, travel to the International Space Station orbiting high above the earth. Look down and what do you see? Unmoving continents, unchanging islands, steady seas and lakes, and so forth. The geologic changes that we observe close-up are relatively minor when viewed from space. The point is, there is a remarkable stability to our planet. We rely on that stability as we buy property, build houses, defend borders, and plan for the future.

The earth's stability is not just a happy accident. The stability we observe was woven into our planet by the Creator. Natural calamities happen and geologic features wear down, but not to the point of obliterating the stability established by God.

Without knowing that God "established the earth, and it stands," we might live in a constant state of uncertainty, hoping that the geology of our world, which seems stable for now, will not suddenly undergo a calamitous change. Of course, if we believe the Bible's predictions about the end times, we know that there will indeed be global calamitous, geologic changes then. But until then we are confident that the earth will remain steady because we know that God is eternally steady, and He built steadiness into this world.

Psalm 119:89-91 summarizes the creation story. The mention of "Your word" in verse 89 is a reference to the fact that by God's word the heavens and earth were created. And His word is immutable. Then verse 90 tells us poetically that global stability is a metaphor for the Lord's faithfulness. Or, looking at it the other way around, the Creator's faithfulness is the reason for the earth's stability. Once again, creation points to a Creator. This is not an unstable, morphing world, and He is not an unstable, morphing God. And, because God is always faithful, we know that His steadfast faithfulness lies behind the stability of the earth. Finally verse 91 tells us the reason for the stability – everything, animate and inanimate, operates according to God's "ordinances," which includes both His moral law and the laws of nature which He established. Furthermore, everything is His servant, and therefore under His command.

Obviously, natural disasters occur, such as landslides, storms, volcanoes, and droughts, and these things cause changes in the landscape. We also should remember that God is not caught off-guard by these events, and that they are directly or indirectly the consequence of sin, and that they do not change the truth of Psalm 119:89-91. The Lord has sovereignly put limits on how much damage they can do. Ultimately, until the end of earth history, our hope and trust is in the faithful, changeless Creator who gave us a stable world as a model of His faithfulness.

RESPOND TO IT

1. Do you think it is possible that the earth, or significant portions of it, might be wiped out by some natural calamity, such as being struck by a comet, a massive earthquake, or some other such thing?

2. Psalm 119:89-91 does not tell us that natural calamities are no big deal. To what degree do you worry about natural disasters? How does Psalm 119:89-91 help put that into perspective?

3. On a piece of paper, illustrate Psalm 119: 89-91.

49
GEOLOGY
Round Up

Creation matters because it connects general revelation and special revelation.

Job 26:7
"He stretches out the north over empty space
And hangs the earth on nothing.

Job 26:10
"He has inscribed a circle on the surface of the waters
At the boundary of light and darkness.

Psalm 19:6
[The sun's] rising is from one end of the heavens,
And its circuit to the other end of them;
And there is nothing hidden from its heat.

Proverbs 8:27
"When He established the heavens, I was there,
When He inscribed a circle on the face of the deep,

Isaiah 40:22
It is He who sits above the circle of the earth,
And its inhabitants are like grasshoppers...

It's remarkable that anyone who believes the Bible would have ever thought that the earth is flat. Amazingly some people still believe it, and a few well-intentioned people (are they Christians?) use biblical metaphors, such as "the ends of the earth," to try to make their case. Their attempts to use such metaphors to prove a flat earth stretch credibility past the breaking point. The verses quoted above are sufficient to show that the Bible has always taught that the earth is a sphere like the moon and sun. We do not need to believe in creation to know that the earth is round, and on this point the Bible and science are in agreement.

Similarly, no Bible-believer should have ever believed mythological stories about the earth resting on the back of a mysterious cosmological creature or on some other kind of literal physical foundation. As early as the book of Job it was well-known that the earth hangs "on nothing." Not much was known about astronomy at that time, but people did know that the earth hangs in space, not on a literal foundation, and they did not believe the ancient myth that the earth floats on a giant ocean.

These observations are important for Christians for a few reasons. First, they show that the Bible and science are not necessarily adversaries. When good science and responsible Bible interpretation meet, they are compatible. So, for Christians, science itself is not an enemy. Second, the Bible explains and affirms what we observe and does not contradict it, provided we make accurate observations and careful biblical interpretations. Third, the verses quoted above invite us to explore the things that they tell us. When God brings up a topic, He opens the door for us to pursue it, examine it, study it, contemplate it, and learn about it by using our God-given reason and senses. Fourth, since God is the Author of both General Revelation – the created universe – and Special Revelation – the Bible – , there is not and cannot be a contradiction between them. In this regard, as the familiar saying goes, "All truth is God's truth."

Our observations and interpretations may be limited and/or flawed, and this could lead to apparent contradictions, but that should not cause us to jump to premature conclusions that Scripture and science are incompatible. Our modern culture's near-absolute trust in science is not actual science, but "scientism," an alternative faith to Christianity, with scientists as its prophets and priests. Similarly, Christians who trust the Bible but disdain science are actually scorning God's General Revelation. They are practicing something called "biblicism," which takes a good thing, belief in the inspiration and authority of the Bible, and ignores something that the Bible actually teaches, namely that we can and should study the universe that God created, which is what science is all about. The Bible should be our filter for any truth claims and the standard against which we evaluate conclusions drawn from science, but belief in it should not be used as an excuse to reject truths that we discover through God's General Revelation.

History and experience show us that scientists sometimes err in their findings and conclusions, and Bible readers sometimes err in their interpretations and conclusions. We all need a healthy dose of humility and self-doubt because:

(a) We are finite, so none of us knows everything; so we all have more to learn, and

(b) We are sinful, so none of us has flawless knowledge; so we all are susceptible to making errors in our observations and understanding.

In conclusion, both Special Revelation and General Revelation affirm that the earth is round and that the earth hangs in space. We look at these truths and marvel at the wise, powerful God who made everything. We are not just impressed with the created earth, but we are far more impressed with the Creator. Creation matters because it is not merely scientific, but it is especially doxological.

RESPOND TO IT

1. Describe how you view the relationship between science and the Bible.

2. Agree/Disagree: Since God is the Author of both General Revelation (everything in the created universe) and Special Revelation (the Bible), there is not and cannot be a contradiction between them.

3. Agree/Disagree: Modern American Christians are more likely to adopt "scientism" than "biblicism."

50
GEOLOGY
NOT A CHANCE

*Creation matters because it is proof that
God left nothing to chance or random forces.*

Psalm 74:16-17

16*Yours is the day,*
Yours also is the night;
You have prepared the light and the sun.
17*You have established all the boundaries of the earth;*
You have made summer and winter.

Psalm 89:11-12, 52

11*The heavens are Yours, the earth also is Yours;*
The world and all it contains,
You have founded them.
12*The north and the south,*
You have created them;
Tabor and Hermon shout for joy at Your name...
52*Blessed be the LORD forever! Amen and Amen*

The psalms go beyond mere assertions; they rejoice in what they assert. While our hearts cannot rejoice in what our heads doubt or reject, our hearts can, and should, rejoice in what our heads know to be true, especially truths about the Lord and what He has done. The psalms' unrestrained joy over creation is a strong statement of the psalmists' complete confidence in the truths that they assert.

A person does not need to be a Bible-believing Christian to know that there is night and day, north and south, summer and winter, land and sea, and earth and heavens. These things are obvious to everyone. Differences of viewpoint enter in when we look for explanations. There are several possible perspectives, and the table below helps identify them:

	God Did it	Nature Did it	Both did it	Don't know, Don't care
Non-Christian	1	2	3	4
Christian	5	6	7	8

Most people can place themselves in one of these eight categories. The non-Christian ought to observe all of creation and conclude that a powerful, glorious God made it all (#1). Many do conclude this, but may or may not come to faith in the triune God of the Bible. Many others are not sure or don't care, so they just look the other way (#4). Additionally, there are many who follow the inclinations of their hearts and reject the possibility of a Creator and view all of creation through a naturalistic lens (#2). Finally, there are a few non-Christians who believe that perhaps there is a divine being who was somehow involved in creation, but he was in some way a partner with nature which was the real guiding force in the creation of the universe (#3).

Most Christians would place themselves in category #5. Many, however, would identify with #7, but unlike their non-Christian counterparts, they believe that God was the real guiding force. They will debate with each other over how and when God did it, but they will agree with the Nicene Creed that God is the "Maker of heaven and earth." Because of the Nicene Creed's affirmation and many biblical assertions, #6 ought not to be a viable option for a Christian who believes the Bible.

Christians also ought to agree that the Bible speaks definitively about our origin, that it tells us everything that we need to know about creation, although it does not tell us everything. So, we explore and study. We may come to different viewpoints, but that can be healthy if we are willing to talk to each other and learn from each other. One category that I believe God does not want Christians to be in is #8. Hundreds of times the Scriptures refer to the Creator and Maker and to specific aspects of creation...after Genesis 1 and 2. Creation matters to God, it mattered to the writers of the Bible, and it should matter to us. It is not just one more data point about God, but it is the basic first thing we should know about Him. Strip it away, and all other theology begins to crumble, becoming vague, disjointed, academic, and even pointless. If we ignore creation, we end up speaking about God no differently than religious-minded non-Christians.

There are two tandem truths that set Christianity apart from all other religions – creation and the incarnation. Both reveal who God is and that He has a plan – He's left nothing to chance or to random forces. Regarding creation, God made the world through His eternally begotten Son Jesus Christ. Regarding the incarnation, God took on humanity in the form of His eternally begotten Son, the God-Man Jesus Christ, who lived on earth in recorded history, died, was buried, rose from the dead, ascended to heaven, and reigns eternally at God's right hand.

The heavens announce the Creator. Jesus reveals Him. Creation tells us what this world is. Jesus tells us who God is. We are fallen, and we have brought down creation with us. Jesus is restoring and reconciling us, and consequently the world around us.

RESPOND TO IT

1. Which of the categories in the table above defines you?

2. Agree/Disagree: Our hearts cannot rejoice in what our heads doubt or reject.

3. Agree/Disagree: If we ignore creation, we end up speaking about God no differently than religious-minded non-Christians.

BOOKENDS OF HISTORY

The Bible views all of human history as taking place within a specific time-frame, one that had a definite beginning and will have a definite conclusion. In Scripture that end is often linked to the beginning. We cannot understand where we are unless we know where we came from and where we are going. Creation addresses where we came from, and it lays the groundwork for understanding where we are going. The final two studies examine these two bookends of life on planet earth.

51

BOOKENDS OF HISTORY

Baseline

*Creation matters because it is the
first bookend of human history.*

When you measure the size of a room, you secure the end of a tape measure to one side and then stretch the tape across the room. The distance to the other side is with reference to the starting point. The Bible repeatedly treats creation as that starting point. In doing so it enables us to determine where we are now and where we are headed.

Creation is more than an isolated doctrine in Scripture. It is the reference point for all of human history. The Scripture writers could have used any other truth about God or some other historical event to make their point, but they consistently referred back to creation. They did this throughout the Old and New Testaments, from Genesis through Revelation.

Creation is not the only truth that the Bible's writers used as a reference point, but it is the most frequent and, arguably, the most significant. The Bible does not permit us to look at Genesis 1 and 2 as a pleasant creation story that we can conveniently leave behind as we move on to more significant historical narratives, more relevant theology, and more practical promises and exhortations. It repeatedly turns our attention back to those chapters and the fact that we are created beings, residing on a created planet, in a created universe. All events in human history are painted in the frame of original creation. Even as the end of the world approaches, the Bible keeps referring back to creation.

Creation places an initial boundary, or bookend, on human history. The Bible does not speak of an indefinite past, nor does it present a vague or gradual beginning. At some specific moment in the past a full-blown universe sprang into being out of nothing. That moment, the initial creation of earth, is the Bible's reference point for documenting human history and articulating many basic doctrines.

STARTING WITH CREATION AS THE INITIAL BASELINE, THE BIBLE:

1. RECORDED THE GROWTH OF ADAM AND EVE'S FAMILY.

Genesis 5:1-4

1This is the book of the generations of Adam. In the day when God created man, He made him in the likeness of God. 2He created them male and female, and He blessed them and named them Man in the day when they were created. 3When Adam had lived one hundred and thirty years, he became the father of a son in his own likeness, according to his image, and named him Seth. 4Then the days of Adam after he became the father of Seth were eight hundred years, and he had other sons and daughters.....

2. AFFIRMED THE SIGNIFICANCE OF HUMAN BEINGS AS MADE IN GOD'S IMAGE.

Genesis 9:6

"Whoever sheds man's blood, By man his blood shall be shed, For in the image of God He made man.

3. REMINDED ISRAEL OF GOD'S PROVIDENTIAL CARE OVER MANKIND.

Deuteronomy 4:31-32

31For the LORD your God is a compassionate God; He will not fail you nor destroy you nor forget the covenant with your fathers which

He swore to them. 32Indeed, ask now concerning the former days which were before you, since the day that God created man on the earth, and inquire from one end of the heavens to the other. Has anything been done like this great thing, or has anything been heard like it?

4. COMPARED THE PERMANENCE OF GOD'S SANCTUARY TO THE PERMANENCE OF THE CREATED WORLD.

Psalm 78:69

And He built His sanctuary like the heights,
Like the earth which He has founded forever.

5. DEFINED THE NATURE OF MALES AND FEMALES.

Mark 10:6

But from the beginning of creation, God made them male and female.

6. PREPARED US FOR THE CLIMACTIC DAYS TO COME AT THE END OF HUMAN HISTORY.

Mark 13:19

For those days will be a time of tribulation such as has not occurred since the beginning of the creation which God created until now, and never will.

7. EXPLAINED THE GOD OF THE GOSPEL TO UNBELIEVERS.

Acts 14:15

and saying, "Men, why are you doing these things? We are also men of the same nature as you, and preach the gospel to you that you should turn from these vain things to a living God, who made the heaven and the earth and the sea and all that is in them.

8. EXPLAINED THE MYSTERY OF SALVATION IN CHRIST IN HISTORICAL PERSPECTIVE.

Ephesians 3:9-11

9and to bring to light what is the administration of the mystery which for ages has been hidden in God who created all things; 10so that the manifold wisdom of God might now be made known through the church to the rulers and the authorities in the heavenly places. 11This was in accordance with the eternal purpose which He carried out in Christ Jesus our Lord,

9. ASSERTED THE DEITY AND MAJESTY OF CHRIST.

Colossians 1:16-17

16For by Him all things were created, both in the heavens and on earth, visible and invisible, whether thrones or dominions or rulers or authorities—all things have been created through Him and for Him. 17He is before all things, and in Him all things hold together.

10. ASSURED US THAT EVEN AS THE WORLD WILL FALL APART IN THE END DAYS, GOD IS IN COMPLETE AND UNSHAKEABLE CONTROL.

Revelation 4:11

"Worthy are You, our Lord and our God, to receive glory and honor and power; for You created all things, and because of Your will they existed, and were created."

Revelation 10:6

and swore by Him who lives forever and ever, who created heaven and the things in it, and the earth and the things in it, and the sea and the things in it, that there will be delay no longer,

Revelation 14:7

and he said with a loud voice, "Fear God, and give Him glory, because the hour of His judgment has come; worship Him who made the heaven and the earth and sea and springs of waters."

Every point on the above list deserves a lengthy discussion. Also, there are other passages in Scripture that use creation as a historical reference point. This simple list is merely intended to demonstrate the important fact that creation mattered greatly to the biblical authors as they taught doctrine and recalled events throughout human history. The Bible explained all of these by referring to creation.

Mark 13:19 contains two additional truths that we should note – *"For those days will be a time of tribulation such as has not occurred since the beginning of the creation which God created until now, and never will."* First, it was Jesus who was speaking in the passage, and it was He who mentioned creation. Christ Himself affirmed the doctrine of creation. If we believe in Jesus as our Lord and Savior, it follows that we also must believe in creation. Also, He emphasized "creation" by adding the words "which God created." He did not want us to be neutral on the question of creation. Our Lord wants us to be settled on the fact that we reside in a world that has one Source – God, and God alone. Jesus believed in creation. Second, He reiterated the familiar refrain "the beginning." In making this reference to Genesis 1:1 Jesus affirmed the Genesis creation account. He also affirmed the truth that there was no pre-existing matter or energy prior to Genesis 1. That was when everything began.

RESPOND TO IT

1. What difference does it make that there actually is an initial boundary for human history?

2. Creation pervaded the thoughts of the biblical writers, yet modern Christians don't think much about it, apart from the debates on creation vs. evolution. What other doctrines usually occupy our minds?

3. Agree/Disagree: If we believe in Jesus, we are obligated to believe in creation?

4. Select at least one of the ten points from the list in this chapter, and elaborate on why it is important.

52

BOOKENDS OF HISTORY

THE DAYS OF FUTURE PAST

*Creation matters because the second bookend
is directly linked to the first.*

NEW HEAVENS AND A NEW EARTH

Isaiah 65:17-19

17"For behold, I create new heavens and a new earth;
And the former things will not be remembered or come to mind.
18"But be glad and rejoice forever in what I create;
For behold, I create Jerusalem for rejoicing
And her people for gladness.
19"I will also rejoice in Jerusalem and be glad in My people;
And there will no longer be heard in her
The voice of weeping and the sound of crying.

2 Peter 3:13

But according to His promise we are looking for new heavens and a
new earth, in which righteousness dwells.

Revelation 21:1

Then I saw a new heaven and a new earth; for the first heaven and
the first earth passed away, and there is no longer any sea.

The Unveiling

Romans 8:18-22

18For I consider that the sufferings of this present time are not worthy to be compared with the glory that is to be revealed to us. 19For the anxious longing of the creation waits eagerly for the revealing of the sons of God. 20For the creation was subjected to futility, not willingly, but because of Him who subjected it, in hope 21that the creation itself also will be set free from its slavery to corruption into the freedom of the glory of the children of God. 22For we know that the whole creation groans and suffers the pains of childbirth together until now.

Wrap-Up

Revelation 10:6-7

6 and swore by Him who lives forever and ever, who created heaven and the things in it, and the earth and the things in it, and the sea and the things in it, that there will be delay no longer, 7but in the days of the voice of the seventh angel, when he is about to sound, then the mystery of God is finished, as He preached to His servants the prophets.

The biblical writers looked ahead to a climactic end of the earth and human history. This will not be a gradual process, but will come rather quickly at the conclusion of a very tumultuous period of time. There was a definite beginning to everything, and there will be a definite end. Just as God controlled the first, so He will control the last. Both are relatively brief events in the overall scope of human history.

Each reference to new heavens and new earth is a look back to Genesis 1:1 – *"In the beginning God created the heavens and the earth."* Among other things, this is telling us that what lies ahead in a glorious eternal future is not unlike what God created from the beginning.

Throughout the Bible, the Genesis account is affirmed and

reaffirmed. The beginning described in Genesis 1 and 2 is the framework for the new beginning that God will create at the end of time. In prophesying the future eternal new heavens and new earth, Isaiah's use of the words "create," "heavens," and "earth," in that sequence in Isaiah 65:17, rivets the readers' attention to the original creation account where those same words in that same sequence were used. Isaiah was telling us that the new heavens and new earth will definitely be different and glorious, but in some way similar to the original heavens and earth.

The end of time is not isolated from the beginning of time. Rather creation foreshadows it. The doctrine of creation has been a reference point throughout biblical history, and it will be vital at the end of days. The end of all things will usher in a new beginning, modeled on the original beginning. The future heavens and earth will be patterned after the arrangement that has existed from the beginning of creation until now.

The Romans 8 passage is related to this. There, all of creation is personified and is looking forward to a future moment when the current order of things will end and a new glorious order will begin. It is not "nature" or "earth" that anticipates a glorious future, but "creation" hopes and longs for it. Everything on this planet is in league with the human inhabitants, and the earth's future is inseparably linked to the human future – glory and freedom from suffering and corruption.

Finally, the Revelation 10:6-7 passage takes us to the same "days of future past" idea. In verses like this, we could easily slide past the references to creation unless we think about what else could have been said. In Revelation 10:6, God's sovereignty could have been mentioned, or His power, or His judgment, or His holiness, or many other things. Yet, here in this verse it is God the Creator who will move things along without delay in the final days.

The message is this: From start to finish, the Lord is in control. He controls events. He controls natural processes. He controls everything because He made everything and He owns everything. He began it all, and He will end it all.

RESPOND TO IT

1. How are the end of the world and the beginning of the world related?

2. Complete this sentence: The end is coming, therefore
   _____ .

Our faith is not in a generic God, but in the Creator God, which is affirmed in the Nicene Creed:

We believe in one God,

the Father, the Almighty,

maker of heaven and earth,

of all that is, seen and unseen.

We believe in one Lord, Jesus Christ,

the only Son of God,

eternally begotten of the Father,

God from God,

Light from Light,

true God from true God,

begotten, not made,

of one being with the Father.

Through him all things were made.

For us and for our salvation

he came down from heaven:

by the power of the Holy Spirit

he became incarnate from the Virgin Mary,

and was made man.

For our sake he was crucified under Pontius Pilate;

he suffered death and was buried.

On the third day he rose again

in accordance with the Scriptures;

he ascended into heaven
and is seated at the right hand of the Father.

He will come again in glory to judge the living and the dead,
and his kingdom will have no end.

We believe in the Holy Spirit, the Lord, the giver of life,
who proceeds from the Father and the Son.
With the Father and the Son he is worshiped and glorified.
He has spoken through the Prophets.
We believe in one holy catholic and apostolic Church.
We acknowledge one baptism for the forgiveness of sins.
We look for the resurrection of the dead,
and the life of the world to come.

Amen.

APPENDIX
How Long

My primary intention in this book has been to establish why the doctrine of creation is extremely important, both in the Bible and to Christians. Secondarily, I have intended to identify aspects of creation on which Christians ought to agree, if they believe that the Bible is inspired and trustworthy.

As I noted in the Introduction, many Christians do not think much about creation apart from the debates about evolution. That is unfortunate because creation is basic to the Christian faith and is foundational to the teaching of most of the Bible. A person cannot claim to hold to the Christian faith and simultaneously deny that God is the Creator.

I hold to the young earth position. For several years after I became a Christian I believed that all life on this planet is the result of evolution, and that God oversaw the process. I struggled to harmonize that view with what I read in Scripture and eventually was persuaded to embrace the young earth model. I believe that the earth, all life, and everything in the heavens were created in six literal 24-hour days, sometime in the relatively recent cosmological past.

Whatever your position on that topic, I hope you have found the 52 studies in this book to have been written in a way that is encouraging to your faith in our Creator.

My goal has been to affirm with Saint Augustine:

"In the beginning, that is from Yourself, in Your wisdom which is begotten of Your substance, You made something and made it out of nothing...Out of nothing You made heaven and earth." [1]

---

1. "Saint Augustine Confessions," Oxford University Press, Oxford World's Classics, 1998, p. 249

Made in the USA
Las Vegas, NV
22 October 2021